WHITETAIL WISDOM

A Proven **12-Step Guide** To Scouting Less and Hunting More

SLOTT ZOELLICK

Daniel E. Schmidt

©2005 Daniel E. Schmidt
Published by

kp books

An Imprint of F+W Publications

700 East State Street • Iola, WI 54990-0001
715-445-2214 • 888-457-2873

Our toll-free number to place an order or obtain
a free catalog is (800) 258-0929.

Library of Congress Catalog Number: 2005924829
ISBN: 0-87349-946-8

Designed by Paul Birling
Edited by Dan Shideler and Joel Marvin

Cover Illustration by Scott Zoellick

Printed in United States of America

For Tracy and Taylor, my guiding lights.

You keep me grounded and constantly remind me
what's most important in this life.

About the Author

Daniel Schmidt was named editor of *Deer & Deer Hunting* in January 2002, becoming only the fourth person to hold that title in the magazine's history. Schmidt fulfilled a lifelong dream to work for *Deer & Deer Hunting* when he became the magazine's associate editor in 1995. He has hunted white-tailed deer for more than 20 years. Each year, he hunts whitetails with his bow, rifle, shotgun and muzzleloader. He has hunted whitetails in 11 states and three Canadian provinces. Besides his work on *D&DH*, Schmidt has edited eight books, including *25 Years of Deer & Deer Hunting: The Original Stump Sitters Magazine*. He has also appeared on several national deer hunting videos, television shows and radio programs. Schmidt and his wife, Tracy, make their home in Iola, Wis., the self-proclaimed "Bowhunting Capital of the World." They have one daughter, Taylor Grace.

Contents

Acknowledgments

Although I had always dreamed about writing a deer-hunting book, the thought never crossed my mind until I neared my 10-year anniversary of working for the nation's top whitetail hunting magazine. *Deer & Deer Hunting* has always attracted the types of writers, photographers and, most importantly, readers who literally eat, breathe and sleep deer hunting. It was those years of interactions with other whitetail fanatics – and several successful seasons in between – that refined my previous 15 years of deer-hunting experience and gave me the skills and confidence to truly begin to understand why deer do what they do when they do it.

I consider myself a hunter's hunter. I will never know it all, and I certainly realize there are many other guys out there who are much better deer hunters right now than any outdoor writer could ever pretend to be. With that in mind, don't believe everything you read in the popular press. Some writers would like you to believe they have all the answers because they have hunted all over the country and killed some big deer. What they don't say is that those hunts are often bought and paid for by someone else and that they merely crawled into a stand that an outfitter hung weeks in advance. It's easy for a skilled hunter to go where the big deer are, kill a few, then drone on and on about how he outsmarted them. It's something completely different to learn how deer behave, then outsmart them while, as I like to say, "chumping it up" with everyone else on highly pressured public land or a small private woodlot near your home.

The real deer-hunting experts are guys who can kill deer on their own, and do it through hard work and determination, not through a fat wallet or a friend who happens to be a land baron. I've been unbelievably fortunate to have known, and sometimes hunted, with some of these people. For that I feel truly blessed. After all, had they not shared their expertise, I might still be bumbling around the woods. Thankfully, I paid attention and can now apply what I've learned to real-world hunting situations ... and succeed. That's why I wrote this book: to give something back to the sport by helping others increase their whitetail learning curve. So, with that in mind, there are quite a few people I need to thank.

Here's to my parents, Daniel J. and Chrisanthia Schmidt: You always encouraged me to do my best and never give up. Mere words cannot express my love and gratitude.

To *D&DH* Group Publisher Hugh McAloon: It's been almost four years since you handed me the editorial reins of North America's No. 1 deer-hunting magazine. Thank you for the opportunity, and for your continued support.

To *D&DH* Publisher Brad Rucks: Remember when you let me hunt behind your house way back when? Thanks for helping put me on the fast track to bowhunting success! What's more, thanks for your friendship over all these years.

To Charles J. Alsheimer: You are a true friend, and I'm proud to call you a colleague. Your insights into white-tailed deer behavior are second to none. Thank you for your undying support, friendship and guidance.

To Patrick Durkin: My mentor for more than six years. You not only taught me how to do it; you taught me how to do it right.

To the best of the best whitetail minds in North America: John J. Ozoga, Leonard Lee Rue III, Bob Zaiglin, Keith McCaffery, Ted Nugent, Walt Hampton, R.G. Bernier, Jack Brauer, Al Hofacker and Rob Wegner. You all have influenced me so much, and I am forever grateful for your constant support.

Here's to my friends and industry insiders: Brian Lovett, Gordy Krahn, Ryan Gilligan, Al and Jennifer West, Craig and Neil Dougherty, Gary Clancy, Doug Below, Bill Marchel, Bryce Towsley, Dave Henderson, Scott Bestul, Jerry Petersen, Gary Sefton, Mark and Terry Drury, Will Primos, Brad Harris, Andy Swift, Jim Casada, Tes and Ron Jolly, John Phillips, Mary Lane (and the spirits of Lois and Reuben Edminster), Jack and Rosie Bazile, Dave Larsen, Walt Larsen, Bart Landsverk, John Trout Jr., Bill Vaznis, Laura Seitz, Claudio Ongaro, Tom Indrebo, Greg Miller, Steve Bartylla, Kevin Howard, Mike Capps, Mike Jordan, Ray, Steve and Wilson Scott, Rodney Dyer, Ray Eye, Dave Samuel, Brian Murphy, C.J. Winand, Keane Maddy, Ray McIntyre, Ronnie "Cuz" Strickland, Dodd Clifton, Ray Lynch, Joe Arterburn, Mark Nelsen, David Draper, Nino Bosaz, Tom Carpenter, Bob Robb, Dave and Mark Beauchaine, Aaron McCullough, Sara and Eric Knapp, Joe Shead, Jake Edson, Jim Schlender, Paul Wait, Susie Melum, Connie Kostrezwa, Pat Boyle, Brian Kruger, Kathy Quinlan, Karen Glinski, Cindi Phillips, Ted Willems, Dave Mueller, Craig Netzer, Jeromy Boutwell, Kevin Ulrich, Karen Knapstein, and Frank and Barbara Schubert. I'd also like to thank Buddy Redling and Bob Lemke for letting me get my foot in the door at Krause Publications in 1994, and Debbie Knauer for giving me a chance to work on *D&DH* shortly thereafter.

Special thanks go to renowned whitetail hunter and TV personality Pat Reeve for supplying several photos for this book.

Thanks are also owed to my brothers and sisters: Roger, Bonnie, Tony, Julie, Ken and Donna. And to my best friend, Joe Peil, and brother-in-law, Scott Chappell, and the now-famous Coffee Lake Hunting Club. Also to the great Schmidt Family hunters past and present: Clarence Schmidt, Eugene Schmidt, Joe Schmidt, Tom Kurth, and to Harvey and Leslie Schmidt for sharing their farm with a clumsy teenager.

Also to the great folks at F+W Publications: Debbie Bradley, Joel Marvin, Don Gulbrandsen, Steve Smith and Paul Birling. Your help in getting this book to print is greatly appreciated.

Finally, and most importantly, here's to every *Deer & Deer Hunting* reader who has called me, sent a letter or e-mail, or stopped me on the street to extend praise, criticism or merely a hunting story. You are the people I work for, and the ones who keep that eternal flame burning deep within my hunter's heart.

Daniel E. Schmidt
Iola, Wisconsin
Aug. 6, 2005

Foreword

Over 25 years ago, I embarked on an incredible journey, one that would change my life forever. In the late 1970s, I left the corporate world to chase my dream of becoming an outdoor writer and nature photographer. The first big break I received in this business was from the owners of *Deer & Deer Hunting* magazine. Over the last quarter century, I've had the distinct privilege of working with the men and women who have made *Deer & Deer Hunting* one of the finest whitetail magazines in the business. The relationships I've made along the way have been special, none more so than the one I've forged with *Deer & Deer Hunting's* current editor, Dan Schmidt. I work with a lot of editors in the publishing business and his expertise in putting together a hunting magazine is second to none. He's also one of the best white-tailed deer hunters in North America.

I first met Dan many years ago when he was young and just starting out in this business. I was in Wisconsin along with the other *Deer & Deer Hunting* field editors to participate in what the magazine called an "editors hunt." Dan and I immediately hit it off, and by the time I left, you would have thought that we were long lost friends. During that hunt, he harvested his first bow buck, and I was able to walk him through the process of photographing it in a natural setting.

What impressed me about Dan was that he was so eager to learn — so hungry for the knowledge we "old staffers" had to share. Now, a decade later, I'm even more impressed that he still has the same eagerness I saw when we first met. No longer is he the new kid on the block. The years of experience he's gained pursuing whitetails across North America and the relationships he's made with some of the biggest names in the deer world have molded him into a sage and savvy whitetail expert.

You are holding a book unlike most whitetail books on the market. It's the journey of an individual who didn't grow up with privilege. What he's learned and accomplished has been done the hard way — primarily on public land and small private parcels, through trial and error. Whether you are just starting out or have years of whitetail hunting experience under your belt, you'll find that *Whitetail Wisdom* will provide you with many new insights into hunting this great animal.

For those just starting out, this book will enable you to flatten your learning curve immensely. One of the struggles I had growing up in the 1950s was that there was no one I could turn to for sound, proven information on hunting white-tailed deer. Consequently, it took me years to learn the ways of the whitetail and how to hunt it. Thanks to books like this, those days are gone.

As you move from chapter to chapter you'll quickly realize that Dan Schmidt is a deer hunter who's "been there" and "done that." Not only does he know white-tailed deer behavior from A to Z, he also knows just about everything about hunting whitetails. You are about to discover that Schmidt is one of those rare individuals who is able to share whitetail wisdom in an easy-to-understand fashion. I've come to realize that his foundation as a person and hunter is rock solid. Consequently, his approach to pursuing the whitetail is one all will appreciate.

You are in for a treat. When you finish this book, you'll find yourself wanting to come back to it time and again.

Charles J. Alsheimer
Northern Field Editor
Deer & Deer Hunting
December 24, 2004

Step 1
Become A Student

What's the key to successful deer hunting? The answer is two-fold: Knowledge makes you powerful, but wisdom provides for consistent success. Highly populated whitetail herds certainly provide opportunities for some hunters to blunder into success here and there, but true whitetail wisdom is what will separate you from the guy who fills his buck tag every few years.

The knowledge end of things involves deer behavior and proven hunting tactics. You'll outsmart more deer, and bigger bucks, when you make the plunge and absorb every written word you can find on those topics. However, you'll enjoy even more consistency when you become wise to what really makes deer tick and begin to understand how environmental factors affect everything from habitat quality to population dynamics. For example, I've long struggled to explain why I'll buy an article to print in *Deer & Deer Hunting* on something as obscure as the reasons why some buck fawns are physically capable of siring offspring. I'll even get occasional calls on such things. "How does that information help me become a better deer hunter?" someone might ask.

I've yet to find the perfect response to that question, and that bothers me a little bit. I guess I can liken the situation to the high schooler who complains to his or her algebra teacher, "When are we ever going to use this in the real world?" when they're struggling with an equation. The answer, of course, is "probably never," but the underlying point is, "the more you know, the more you grow." Therein lies the key to becoming a consistently successful, and more appreciative, deer hunter. The more you know about the flora and the fauna, the more likely you are to enjoy the experience and reap the rewards. And, when making that first step to whitetail hunting success, every hunter needs to again become the student. The best way to start is to learn and understand the important five-point pyramid containing knowledge of weather, food sources, habitat quality, human pressure and deer biology.

Watch the Weather

Most states offer early archery seasons, and in recent years these seasons have featured unseasonably warm weather. While temperatures in the 40s and highs in the 60s make for comfortable tree-stand vigils, they literally shut down daytime deer activity. In fact, the weather's influence on deer activity has been scientifically documented as a major suppressor/stimulator of daytime deer activity.

Over the past 20 years, no one has studied this phenomenon more closely than *Deer & Deer Hunting's* Northern Field Editor Charles Alsheimer. He has written dozens of articles on the topic and even included lengthy explanations of how weather affects deer in his highly acclaimed book, *Hunting Whitetails by the Moon* (Krause Publications, 800-258-0929).

According to Alsheimer, whitetails have a built-in mechanism that can detect impending weather changes. This mechanism allows them to detect falling barometric pressure, and, as a result, dramatically increase their feeding activity before bad weather arrives. Some research biologists might cringe when they hear

◀ **Whitetail knowledge makes you a better hunter, but wisdom is the real key to consistent success.**

Learn how deer use the food sources on the land you hunt, and study their behavior as to how they switch from various food sources throughout the fall.

If you want to see more deer, limit the amount of vehicle traffic and extraneous human activity that take place on your hunting property.

such anecdotal "absolutes," but this point has actually been proven through scientific studies. For example, Illinois biologist Keith Thomas conducted a comprehensive study that concluded most whitetail feeding occurred when the barometric pressure hovered between 29.80 and 30.29 inches, regardless of whether the barometric pressure was rising or falling.

Alsheimer's 30-plus years of studying deer behavior reveal matching observations. "With few exceptions, deer move little during low-pressure fronts, which often result in fog, rain or snow," Alsheimer said. "Then, as fronts pass and the barometer rises, deer activity increases dramatically – if air temperatures match the whitetail's comfort zone."

Air temperature's effect on deer activity goes straight to the phenomenon Alsheimer dubbed as "The Fur Factor," which basically states that deer living north of the 40th parallel shut down when temperatures exceed 45 degrees. "With their heavy fur coats and inability to ventilate as humans do, white-tailed deer simply cannot function in warm weather," he said.

Of course, temperature is relative to region. Whereas Northern deer might be uncomfortable in 50-degree weather, the opposite holds true for whitetails living in, say, some areas of Alabama, South Carolina and Florida's panhandle. It's all

HOW TO BECOME A STUDENT

◊   **Watch the weather.** Whitetails have a built-in mechanism that can detect impending weather changes. This mechanism allows them to detect falling barometric pressure, and, as a result, dramatically increase their feeding activity before bad weather arrives.

◊   **Key in on food sources.** Whitetails eat to live and live to eat. Learn how deer use the food sources on the land you hunt, and study their behavior as to how they switch from various food sources throughout the fall.

◊   **Locate and hunt the thick stuff.** White-tailed deer are crepuscular creatures: They eat and move, for the most part, on the fringe hours of daylight. This secretive nature calls for covert behavior, and such behavior calls for protective cover. Find these areas, and you'll find great ambush locations.

◊   **Take a low-impact approach.** If you want to see more deer, limit the amount of vehicle traffic and extraneous human activity that takes place on your hunting property. This is especially helpful when trying to hunt mature deer. Big bucks will temporarily vacate their core areas when faced with constant intrusions.

◊   **Understand how deer densities work.** Just because the habitat in your county or state is home to 50 or more deer per square mile doesn't mean you will necessarily see a lot of deer while hunting. A density that high still only means that, on average, there are 50 deer for every 640 acres of deer habitat, not every single square mile in the area. What's more, some square miles of habitat might have significantly more deer than others, which means some individual properties might have relatively few deer.

Just because the habitat in your county or state is home to 50 or more deer per square mile doesn't mean you will necessarily see a lot of deer every time you go hunting.

relative, but deer in warmer climates will obviously move more in 50-degree weather if they spend most of the year in scorcher-type environments.

Find Good Groceries

Food availability is another major variable that influences deer behavior. Every year after deer season, I receive nearly the same rally cry from many concerned hunters, "There just aren't that many deer out there; not nearly as many as the game agency says there are. I saw way more deer 20 years ago than I do now."

The concerns are real, but the blame is ill founded. However, I give the hunter the benefit of the doubt, and that's why my first response is to ask him or her to explain their hunting property. Invariably, the hunter explains how he's hunted the same property for 20 years and, back in the beginning, it used to be active farmland or a young stand of clear-cut regrowth. Many additional factors come into play in this example, such as other land-use trends, hunting pressure, suburban development, neighboring properties, etc., but basically, the key to the change in deer use can be directly linked to food availability and the law of diminishing returns. Simply, time marches on, and deer change their habits as food sources change. If a given property continues to produce quality forage, deer will "keep shopping" regardless of the other factors.

The whitetail's triumphant return has caused some problems. Most notably, the habitat is now suffering because too many deer roam the countryside.

Whether it's farm crops like corn, soybeans or alfalfa, or mast crops like acorns, beechnuts or locust pods, food locations dictate how, when and where deer eat, rest and move. Learning the nuances within their seasonal movement behavior isn't always easy because a lot depends on food availability, especially for mast crops. The cyclical nature of mast crop production causes deer to adopt different travel patterns throughout fall, and these patterns can literally change overnight. Whitetails are opportunists in that they gravitate to the best food sources when those foods are in peak production. A good example can be seen each fall in farm country, especially where soybeans are grown. In my home county, it's not uncommon to drive home from work in late August or early September and see 30, 40, and sometimes more, deer in every soybean field. They will devour the tender green shoots and leaves, no doubt unknowingly getting their last big fix of vitamin K before fall marches on. These same deer are practically nowhere to be seen when the soybean fields ripen and turn yellow. When that happens, usually after mid-September, deer shift their focus to the deep-woods mast crops. That's when savvy bowhunters make sure they're perched somewhere along an oak ridge that's dropping its crop of protein-rich deer foods.

Food sources vary widely throughout North America. The Midwest has its acorns and farm crops. The South provides acorns, persimmons, wild plums and lush food plots. The East specializes in apples and beechnuts. But it doesn't matter what foods your land produces. To become a student of the whitetail, you need to learn how, when, where and why deer use these food sources.

People who use research to push trophy-buck agendas are doing it for their own selfish reasons – not for the good of the resource.

Hunt Great Cover

Visualize for a moment the best deer hunting land you've ever hunted. Was it along a wide-open fallow field; in the middle of a park-like woodlot with little understory; or in a tree stand overlooking a dense swamp, thicket or clearcut? I'll bet my best grunt call that it was something similar to the last one: a heck-hole of nasty proportions; a place that looked "bucky" the instant you laid eyes on it.

In this age of shrinking hunting parcels – it seems like we're all pushed onto smaller areas each year – it's easy to throw up your hands and settle for what you have access to. In many cases that means hunting really marginal deer habitat. It also means spending more hours afield while seeing fewer deer. Again, the deer are out there; it's just a matter of gaining access to where they spend most of their time.

This isn't a new dilemma. Ask any old-timer, and they'll tell you to hunt "the thick stuff" if you want to be one of those hunters who always gets his deer. Whitetails prefer thick cover because they are crepuscular creatures: They eat and move, for the most part, on the fringe hours of daylight. This secretive nature calls for covert behavior, and such behavior calls for protective cover.

A common rookie mistake is to locate thick cover and dive into it headfirst. My buddy and I must have made this mistake hundreds of times when we were trying to learn how to hunt a vast national forest in the 1980s. We simply parked our truck at the side of a forest road, blundered off into a swamp or clearcut, and hung our stands after finding some rubs, scrapes or well-worn deer trails. Successfully hunting thick cover, which can be described plurally as travel corridors, requires much more forethought because these are areas that deer use for secure daytime travel.

The best strategy for hunting thick cover is to locate huntable areas, then view an aerial map (see Chapter 6 for more information) and highlight bottlenecks, pinch points or other terrain features. A few minutes of pre-hunt planning will at least put you in the ballpark. From there, it's a matter of observing deer in their natural environment and learning how they move through the cover in daylight.

Deal With Human Pressure

Human pressure – be it from hunters, hikers or horse riders – is the No. 1 suppressor of daytime deer activity. Alsheimer and Vermont biologist Wayne Laroche have documented the extent of this suppressor during their ongoing study of how the moon affects deer behavior. Using trail timers to document deer activity in several states, they learned that 55 percent of all deer movement occurs during daylight in areas where there is little or no human pressure. Throw human pressure into the mix, and the percentage falls way off. For example, the trail-timer data shows that moderate to heavy human activity causes deer to spend only 30 percent of daylight hours moving throughout their home areas.

Extrapolate those figures for what they're worth. Translation: If you're after mature deer, be cautious as to how you use your property. Avoid running ATVs across the property at all times of the day, and adopt a low-impact approach for deer-sensitive zones like bedding and feeding areas throughout the year. Also, it's wise to limit blood-trailing recoveries to the cover of darkness, especially when a wounded deer runs into a self-imposed sanctuary. Mature bucks are especially sensitive to pressure, and it doesn't take much to blow them out of an area. Spook a buck you're hunting more than once, and you probably won't see him during daylight for the rest of the season.

I hesitate to mention these tactics, because it goes against my beliefs that deer hunting should be fun and enjoyable. Hunters shouldn't be so paranoid about spooking deer that they walk through the woods like they're stepping on eggshells. However, nothing will spook a mature deer from its core area more than constant human pressure. Still, human pressure affects the behavior of deer of all ages. Even antlerless deer won't tolerate constant intrusions.

How you approach and leave your stand sites definitely affects deer patterns. When possible, don't walk across open fields to get to or from your stands. If that means walking a quarter-mile out of your way so you can skirt a woodline, do it. You'll see fewer and fewer deer throughout the season if you constantly blow across such feeding areas just to take a shortcut to your stand. Field-side bowhunting is especially difficult in the afternoon, because deer invariably show up before darkness and leave you watching them from a distance. In these situations, it's a

Whereas Northern deer might be uncomfortable in 50-degree weather, the opposite holds true for whitetails living in, say, some areas of the Deep South.

huge mistake to get out of your stand and walk across the field before darkness. They might be 300 yards away, but I guarantee that these deer will remember where you appeared and walked across the field. The best way to combat this problem is to have a partner pick you up after darkness. The intrusion of someone else walking in from the road or driving a vehicle to get you will still spook deer, but not nearly as bad as you will by suddenly appearing in what otherwise is a deer's comfort zone.

As stated, ATVs and other hunting vehicles can upset a deer's travel pattern when they're used throughout the day. Many outfitters, however, have told me over the years that vehicle use spooks fewer deer when the vehicles are used solely for going to and from stands in the darkness of morning and/or evening. Furthermore, deer in farm country are much more tolerant of vehicles, because they see tractors and other farm machinery throughout the year. In fact, on several occasions I've hunted farmland in Illinois and Wisconsin where outfitters used tractors to give me rides to stand locations. The rationale was to approach the stand with a vehicle deer were used to. Don't ask me why or how, but the tactic seemingly works. I used the tactic this past fall and started seeing deer moving about nonchalantly within minutes of jumping off a tractor and climbing into my stand. In fact, my guide wasn't even out of sight when the first deer appeared in a nearby meadow.

Many years ago, whitetail expert Richard Prior penned what I consider the best advice anyone could ever give a deer hunter. He said deer study, no matter what your particular field might be, becomes more and more fascinating as experience accumulates. "If by degrees you find that you can think like the deer, anticipating their movements and trying to understand their way of life, it will become a challenging battle of wits – human brains matched against their finer senses. Never forget the consideration which these lovely animals are due. To us it is just a hobby – to them a life or death struggle for survival in a very hostile world. Much of their ability to survive stems from their ability to watch us without our being aware, and to act accordingly. A good deer watcher should always try to do the same."

Understand Deer Densities

If you've read any magazine articles or watched the popular hunting shows on TV in the past 10 years, you might believe that deer sex ratios – the number of males to females – is so badly skewed across North America that white-tailed bucks are an endangered species. Muddying the waters even more is the fact that nearly every state has areas with basically no quotas on does. Even though extra doe tags might come at cost, commonly $6 to $12 per tag, the constant message is to thin the doe herd.

The trickle-down effect of this "kill-the-deer" mentality is that hunters mistakenly believe does must greatly outnumber bucks. As I write this, I'm merely one week removed from a conversation with a Massachusetts hunter who claimed his state's deer sex ratio was "at least 10 adult does for every antlered buck."

In reality, such adult sex ratios are, for all intents and purposes, impossible to achieve. Ask any biologist, and he'll tell you that a free-ranging deer herd cannot achieve an adult-doe-to-antlered buck ratio much higher than 3-to-1. According to retired biologist Keith McCaffery, who worked for 30 years as a lead deer manager in the Upper Midwest, the only way to achieve adult ratios of 3-to-1 would be for the herd to have minimal, if any, recruitment. In other words, few fawns could be born, and fewer could survive.

"In managed herds that have 'normal' fawn production and survival, the flush of young bucks will replace those shot in the previous hunting season," McCaffery said. "By 'normal' fawn production and survival, I'm suggesting an average of about one fawn per doe. Under the latter system, 100 does would have 100 fawns and slightly over half of these fawns would be bucks."

McCaffery offers a simple exercise to better understand this complex issue. "Take a pencil and paper and assume you start with a pre-hunt fall population of 100 antlered bucks, 100 adult does, and 100 fawns," he explained. "For simplicity's sake, assume there are equal numbers of male and female fawns. Then imagine some kind of harvest scenario that might distort the sex ratio. For example, if *all* antlered bucks were removed and *no* antlerless deer were removed, the adult sex ratio the next fall would be 3-to-1. That is, 50 antlered bucks (100 percent yearlings) and 150 adult does that would produce 150 fawns. This could be repeated ad infinitum and the adult sex ratio would remain 3-to-1, so long as production remained at one fawn per doe. Most reasonable folks know that not *all* antlered bucks are killed each

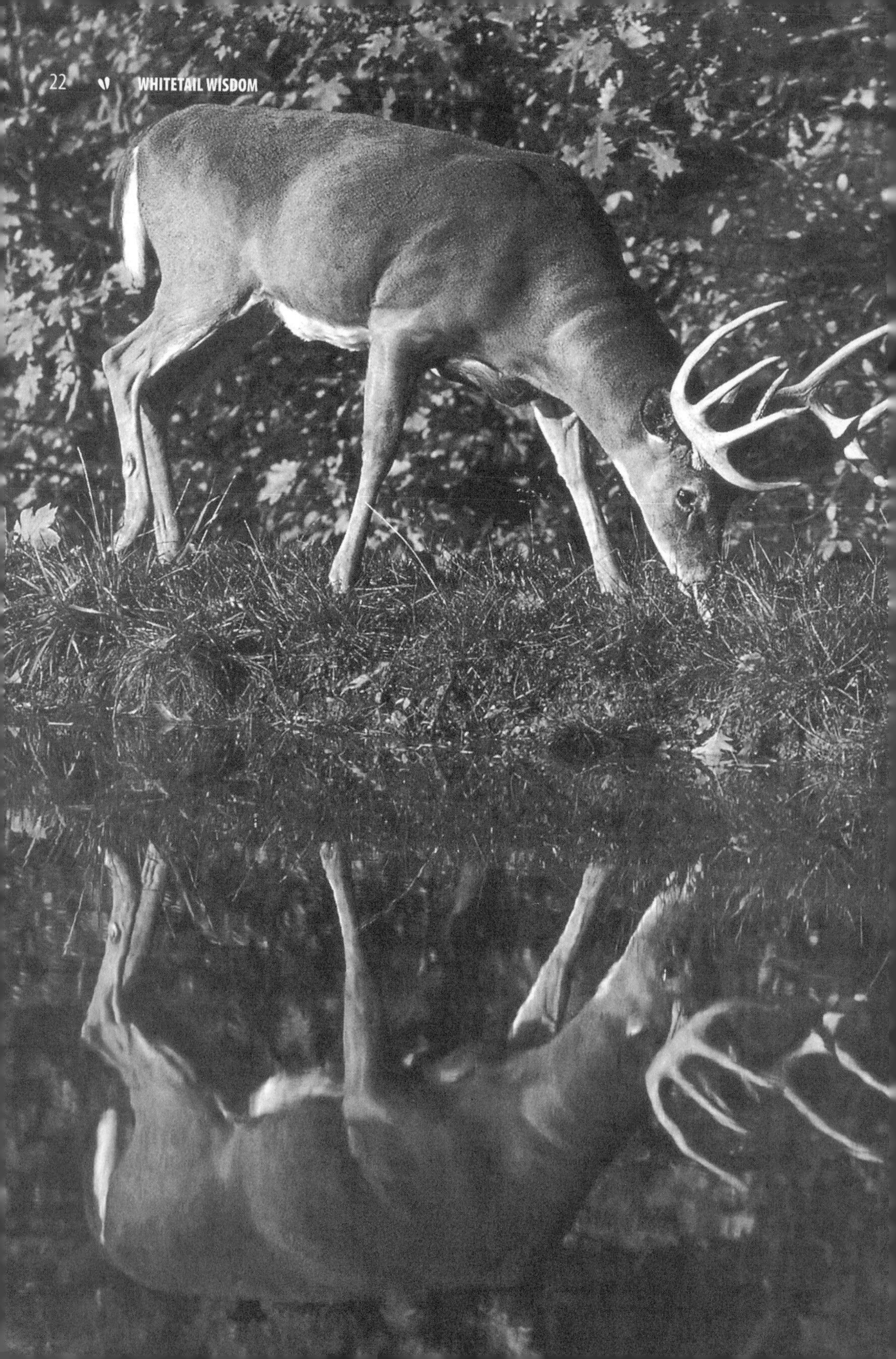

HOW DEER AFFECT OTHER WILDLIFE

❧ As an avid whitetail hunter, you probably live relatively close to your favorite hunting spots and have access to abundant herds. Such was not always the case. In fact, whitetails were relatively scarce at the turn of the last century. Thanks to conservation-minded individuals, we now are reaping the rewards of strict hunting regulations and wise habitat management.

The whitetail's triumphant return, however, has also caused problems. Mostly notably, the habitat is now suffering because too many deer roam the countryside. Browsing whitetails feed on some plants more than others, and that leads to the loss of some woodland browse species, even if only temporarily. This sometimes results in the loss of songbird and small-mammal populations in areas overpopulated by deer. A 1990s study in Pennsylvania, for example, showed that indigo buntings, wood pewees, robins and yellow-billed cuckoos were eliminated from areas where deer densities exceeded 65 deer per square mile of habitat.

Studies in other states have netted similar conclusions. Even more alarming is the fact that other studies have shown that years of overbrowsing have depleted woodlands so badly that it would take centuries for them to regenerate even if deer densities were reduced to prescribed levels immediately. Responsible hunters should heed these warning signs and accept the role as "deer manager consultants." By stepping to the plate and harvesting does early and often, hunters can send a message to nonhunters that they indeed care about protecting and preserving natural resources.

year and that some mortality (hunting, auto accidents, predation, disease, etc.) takes place on the antlerless deer, otherwise herds would quickly spiral out of control. This logic moves the sex ratio to something much less than 3-to-1."

It's important to shed light on this topic because the real problem with deer herds is densities. There are simply too many deer on the landscape, and that's where your role as a responsible hunter comes into play. The very best habitat in North America should not be home to more than 35 deer per square mile (psm). In most areas, densities far exceed that number, and, in some places, densities exceed 100 deer psm. Next, it's important to note that high densities do not mean there are deer behind every tree. Again, it's all relative. What's more, simple math ends when you walk into the woods. Just because the habitat in your county is home to an average of, say, 50 deer psm doesn't mean you will see three deer on your 40-acre hunting parcel every day (50 deer per square mile divided by 16 40-acre parcels equals 3.125). The complex nature of deer behavior clouds such comparisons beyond belief. However, in this case, knowing that you're hunting an area with high deer densities provides you with the assurances you're not hamstringing management efforts (from a scientific standpoint, anyway) if you fill all your doe tags and harvest the occasional buck fawn or yearling buck. People who use research to push trophy-buck agendas are doing it for their own selfish reasons – not for the good of the resource.

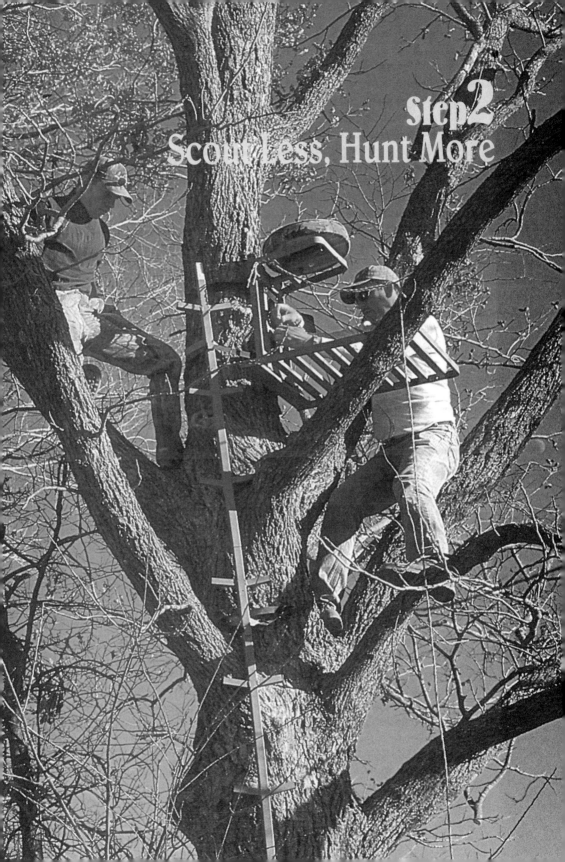

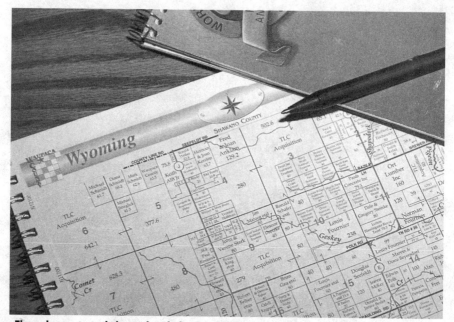

The only way to truly learn deer behavior and travel patterns is to look at your maps and make a few educated guesses, then get out there and see firsthand how deer use your hunting property.

I'm not *that* old, but I remember when the mere sight of a deer track literally sent shivers up my spine. Granted, at the time my family and I hunted the low-density North Woods deer herds. Still, a fresh track in the mud or snow was cause for celebration, hours of "what if" intrigue and, above all, renewed hope for the hunt. That was back in the 1970s – when most deer herds across the nation were still in the recovery stage. Back then, intense post-season scouting was the catch phrase among avid hunters. The serious buck hunters, our heroes, spoke and wrote of scouting as being of utmost importance for success of any kind. A lot has changed since then. Post-season scouting, while still the No. 1 key to consistent success, is more of a hobby for today's whitetail enthusiast. The advent of remote-sensing cameras and the availability of aerial photos and maps via the Internet has taken the game to new levels.

You don't necessarily need an ultra-serious post-season scouting plan to succeed. That's what makes the advice in this chapter possibly unlike anything you've read before. Has deer hunting become easier? Not necessarily. What has happened, however, is that burgeoning deer herds have provided seemingly endless opportunities. What's more, abundant tags and access to quality land – properties built around whitetails – make it easier for hunters to hunt more and scout less. Yes, many of our forefathers must be looking down on us and praying that we all realize how good we have it, compared to what they experienced.

Hands-on scouting is the best way to learn how and why deer do what they do, and when they do it.

Advice From A Pro

When he's not traveling the country promoting bowhunting at sports shows, legendary archer Myles Keller is in the woods scouting for bowhunting season. His philosophy? A whitetail hunter can never have too much information about deer behavior and habits. Being a student of the deer woods helps Keller formulate game plans to outsmart big whitetails with strategic tree stand placement.

"You always have to be one step ahead, especially if you're trophy hunting," Keller once told me. "You have to know where the sign is and where deer will move as the season progresses. The days of sitting blindly and killing big deer ... well, those days are over."

Keller collects a lot of information by glassing crop fields in summer. This tactic has helped him kill many big bucks in undisturbed, low-traffic areas. "The bucks are still in bachelor groups at that time," he said. "That allows you to pick out a deer that really inspires you. Yes, they will probably change their habits by hunting season, but in some areas, the early season is a good time to find a buck, pattern him off the fields in the morning and evening, and determine some setups. In some states, the season is early enough that you can figure out a way to get close to those big deer."

Keller's proven tactics include a conservative approach. He says it's critical to err on the side of caution and to constantly learn more about your hunting land. The key difference here is that hunters should realize that smart scouting doesn't need to

If you must cut shooting lanes on your property, do so after the season to prevent spooking mature whitetails from their core areas.

be exhausting. With some planning and a little bit of legwork, a hunter can quickly assess how deer use the terrain. From there, draw on your topographical maps and note terrain features and deer sign. Major deer runways are easy to find, and they can tell you a lot about deer movement. For example, a runway that connects different cover types, such as oak forests and pine thickets, likely indicates preferred feeding and bedding areas. However, don't be fooled into believing that a well-used deer trail is your ticket to a monster buck. This holds especially true in states where baiting is legal, because major runways are often signs of nighttime activity. Although mature bucks will use these routes during the rut, they seldom travel major runways during daylight early and late in the season.

To outsmart mature deer, key on runways as starting points. From there, scout the area and look for parallel trails. Serious hunters must do a serious job of scouting and researching the land they will be hunting. "You should know the terrain like the back of your hand," according to Keller. With that in mind, the post-season is the best time to scout for new hunting spots. By then, all foliage is off the trees, which makes it easy to identify deer trails, buck rubs, old scrapes, etc.

The best way to get a jump on post-season scouting trips is to acquire topographical maps and aerial photos of your hunting land. These tools can reveal terrain features you might be unaware of, and can indicate funnels and travel corridors that connect potential bedding and feeding areas. Use maps and photos to plan hunts around the changing phases of the deer season. For example, from previous hunts, you might know that deer use certain ridges and benches more during the rut than during the early season. With maps and photos, you can devise a game plan for the early season and the pre-rut. Don't let these tools become crutches, however. Use them to find potential food sources, fence lines and other connecting areas from bedding areas to feeding areas. The key is to plan ahead, not obsess over the ideal spot to place your tree stand. From there, use hunting observations to determine when deer use the various areas (i.e. pinpointing morning vs. evening stand locations).

The Scout-While-Hunting Method

A buck my brother shot years ago provides a good example of how scouting while you're hunting can pay huge dividends during the same season. We had long hunted a vast, nondescript national forest in northern Wisconsin. The deer population was, and still is, very low, and the habitat was terrible, to say the least. As a result, we were constantly looking for new spots within our area. One fall, during the early archery season, I spent the better part of a day speed-scouting a hardwood ridge that tapered off into a river-bottom swamp. The area looked good on paper – the topographical map indicated several natural funnels and pinch points that would certainly dictate deer movement.

The morning after walking the area, I packed in a portable ladder stand and erected it within 100 yards of two major trail crossings. I sat for several hours and watched as deer after deer worked their way up the river bottom and cruised a side hill on the hardwood ridge. I also noted how three different bucks skirted the trails. Instead of following the runways, they used faint parallel trails that wound through a small but dense spruce patch. I knew the spruce corridor would be a great spot for the gun season, but I also knew (from surveying the area with my binoculars while hunting) that tree-stand hunting wouldn't be an option. After hunting the area several more times that week, I concluded the spruce grove was definitely a "morning spot."

When gun season arrived, I told my brother he should hunt the spot because he hadn't shot a buck in a few years and that it would make me happiest if he got the first chance. Armed with nothing more than his rifle and a 5-gallon bucket, he worked his way into the spruce thicket before first light and set up in a small clearing. To his surprise, but certainly not mine, a dandy 8-pointer appeared shortly after daybreak. He killed it cleanly with a 40-yard shot. That area received very little hunting pressure, and I honestly believe that buck had never encountered a hunter in that grove before. We could have probably pinpointed that spot by spending many hours dissecting the area during post-season scouting trips. However, we wouldn't have known how deer used the grove had I not bowhunted the area and observed firsthand exactly when and where deer appeared.

We are all so busy these days that the scout-while-hunting method is really the only tactic we use to find new spots and learn more about other mostly unfamiliar properties. I use the tactic a lot while turkey hunting public land in spring. I'm surprised at how much I can learn about a local deer herd during just one day of chasing gobblers. Best of all, I don't have to worry if I spook deer, because deer season is, after all, usually five months away.

By learning how does use their home ranges, hunters can easily predict their movements, because does typically have much smaller home ranges than bucks.

When using this approach, it's wise to maintain a detailed hunting journal. Draw crude maps, and note all the obvious things like trails, rubs and scrapes. Also note the less-subtle signs, such as converging terrain features, inside corners, stream crossings, etc. The more detail you record, the better prepared you'll be when trying to match wits with wary whitetails.

Mastering Whitetail Bedrooms

It's difficult, if not impossible, for consistently successful buck hunters to pinpoint big-buck bedding areas. Each situation is different, and it takes hours of pre-season scouting for hunters to unravel big-buck secrets. For example, experts such as Myles Keller of Minnesota and Greg Miller of Wisconsin typically search for buck bedding areas after deer season because they want to cause as little disturbance as possible in the buck's core area.

Hunters must be careful not to spread their scent through an area while scouting. You should be able to scout for several hours in the post-season without worrying about educating mature bucks too much. It might take a few trips, but a hunter can get a good grasp of a buck's home range by learning as much as he can about the deer's bedding areas. In fact, many of the highly seasoned buck hunters won't even consider hunting a property until they scout and know every inch of the terrain. I'm not one of them, but the tactic is certainly sound. They key, in my opinion, is

**The most successful hunters are those who adopt an aggressive approach and never let up
– no matter how tough the hunting gets.**

to know basic terrain features and precisely how wind currents will affect certain stand sites. In fact, wind direction should be your No. 1 concern. If you're going to be successful, you have to have a stand site for every possible wind direction. Never hunt a stand when wind conditions are not favorable. If you do, you're bound to spook mature bucks and will probably never see them during shooting hours.

A good example of how to approach a bedding area is to imagine your hunting land includes an oak ridge with bedding areas to the east and west. If the predominant wind comes from the southwest, hunt the ridge's northeastern corner. If winds shift, hunt the western corner if your scent doesn't blow into the bedding area. Also, remember that while a stand might be positioned correctly for wind direction, the route to it might not be. It's important to have more than one route to each stand. The alternative route might require walking twice as far, but the result -- an undetected approach -- will be worth it. "You're less likely to be patterned by using this approach," Keller told me. "I have killed quite a few bucks with a cross-wind approach. This requires you to have a pretty good handle on the directional movement of the deer in your area."

Stand Placement Tips

Finding prime areas to intercept bucks is only part of the equation. Tree stand placement is critical to success. This is where many hunters fail. After selecting a stand site, do not cut large shooting lanes, trim low-hanging branches or make other obvious alterations a wary buck might notice, because they will notice it and alter their behavior accordingly. If you must make shooting lanes, be subtle and do it after the season. Trim just enough overhanging branches to give yourself a

When deer "disappear" from early season locations, go deeper into the woods and find productive mast trees.

small opening here and there around your stand. I seldom use a pruning saw to cut shooting holes. Instead, I find a dead branch and use it to whack down live branches here or there. Instead of breaking down saplings, I bend them down or around another tree to create openings. This provides natural shooting openings that deer seldom, if ever, notice.

Also, if you must clear shooting lanes, do it after hunting season. Make cuts to saplings and brush as close to the ground as possible, leaving no signs of stumps or fresh cuts. If you follow these guidelines and perform these tasks, say, in January, February or March, I wouldn't worry about spending a few hours in the hunting area. In fact, if your main goal is to simply create good deer hunting spots, spend as much time as needed. However, if your goal is to hunt mature deer, try to get in and out without altering the landscape too much. That brings me to a much-needed point: Don't be so concerned about spooking deer that you're afraid to go in the woods. This type of self-inflicted anxiety runs rampant among today's hunters, because many guys are so worried about spooking "their" deer onto neighboring properties. Mature bucks are wary creatures, but I can relate scores of instances where blundering hunters kill them after basically remodeling their woodlots. The key is to have fun out there … not to let the pre-season preparations get you all stressed out.

Regardless of how careful you are with scent control, you will invariably leave some scent wherever you walk in the woods. Therefore, stands should be hung in trees that provide exceptional background cover. Do not hang stands in mature trees that offer few, if any, branches as a backdrop for breaking up your outline. Also, don't expect your stand site to offer shots in every direction. Study the site and err on the side of camouflage. Place your stand so it leaves a couple of shooting options. You might get a second chance at a buck that passes your stand unaware of you. If a second shooting lane isn't available and the deer gets by you, commit him to memory because it might be the last time you see that deer. Mature bucks seldom make the same mistake twice.

Depending on the tree, hang your stand at a height that is comfortable for you. Remember, height isn't as important as camouflage. Many hunters consistently kill big bucks from stands at heights less than 14 feet. Again, it is critical to stay hidden and place stands to take advantage of wind. One of my most productive stands over the years is a spot where I can only hang my stand 12 feet off the ground. This spot is so productive because it faces due west, and that hunting property usually experiences west winds. Also, the tree, a red oak, is shadowed by a 16-foot-high fir. The thick evergreen grew in a way that allowed me to clip just a couple branches and use it for total concealment while I'm sitting in the oak. My head and shoulders are literally the only parts of my body that can be seen from the ground. It's a great ambush location because a classic rub line winds past that fir. As a result, I've killed many bucks from that spot.

All aspects of tree-stand placement – where, when and how high – should account for hunting pressure. As a rule, place your stand at least one month before the season starts. Although many seasoned bowhunters prefer to hunt high – 22 to 25 feet is common – heights of 15 to 20 feet are equally effective at breaking up your outline if there is good background camouflage.

HOW TO SCOUT LESS AND HUNT MORE

❧ **Scout with a purpose.** Glass field edges from the road and hunt fringe areas of your property. Make mental notes of how deer use the property, even when they are off in the distance. The more you learn about deer behavior, the better prepared you'll be when hanging stands.

❧ **Analyze everything.** An old-time carpenter's saying states, "Measure twice; cut once." The same idea rings true for whitetail scouting. Don't place your tree stands merely in spots that look good. Spend time in the woods and analyze everything while crouching down (to give you the perspective of a deer) when looking for stand sites. Pick spots that maximize natural camouflage, especially backdrops that provide cover even after leaves fall from the trees.

❧ **Be careful with shooting lanes.** Avoid cutting obvious lanes, because mature deer will quickly notice the changes and avoid these areas in the future. Analyze each potential saw cut by asking yourself, "Is it really necessary?" The best shooting lanes are made by merely bending saplings around other trees and snapping off twigs and limbs that are already dead.

❧ **Think ahead.** Hang stands at least one month before the season starts. It's also wise to hang stands just before a rainstorm. This approach will allow you to get your stand in place and allow the rain to wash away human scent. Likewise, for safety's sake, never hang stands when it's raining. One slip could forever change your life. It's not worth it.

❧ **Be a clock watcher.** Early season sits are most productive around the fringe hours of daylight. Don't waste time on stand in the middle of the day when temperatures exceed 50 degrees. On the other hand, hunt long and hard when the weather turns colder … and when the pre-rut gives way to full-blown rutting activity.

Maintaining an ambush spot's "element of surprise" is the No. 1 key to tree-stand hunting.

Hunting Tactics

A smart hunting approach is the final piece of the puzzle. Although quality stand placement and smart wind tactics place hunters in the ballpark, many hunters fail because they make careless mistakes. Over the years, I've learned not to bowhunt the same stand more than two consecutive days when hunting mature deer. I don't adhere to this rule during gun seasons, however, because pressure on surrounding properties typically keeps deer moving throughout the short gun seasons. The consecutive-day advice, however, is not written in stone, and success does not change my strategies. For example, in 2001 and 2004, I hunted consecutive stands in which I shot a doe one day and a buck the next. That's right: two deer in two days from the same stand ... on two separate occasions! What's more, during both seasons, the bucks appeared the following days despite the fact that I trailed the does and field dressed them in the same general area. I can't prove it, but I attribute both instances to the does being dragged from the woods. The bucks must have smelled these trails and allowed curiosity to get the best of them.

The key to those success stories is that I quickly realized by hunting other areas of the property that those two stand sites would only produce during afternoon vigils. As a result, I hung those stands and only hunted them in the afternoon. In fact, I've hunted that property for nearly a decade now and have never hunted either stand site in the morning. Hunting the same stand mornings and evenings is a mistake many hunters make. I've hunted hundreds of stand sites over the years and can count on one hand the number of spots that were equally productive in mornings and afternoons. Deer behavior is the reason for the disparity. Like people, unpressured deer have routines. They often rest in different areas and use different feeding areas at various times of the day.

The time spent on stand, or lack thereof, is another common mistake. Most guys get so jacked up to go hunting that they arrive at their stands an hour before daylight. The average hunter can't sit still for more than four hours, so that typically means they are out of their stands by 9 or 10 a.m. As a result, they often miss out on the best time to waylay a mature buck, which, especially during the rut, is the midday window that runs from about 10 a.m. to 2 p.m. Much has been written about this topic, and it's important to note that deer activity during this period isn't typically red hot. The difference lies in the ratio of the types of deer you'll commonly see. Ask any seasoned buck hunter, and he'll tell you that if you see a single deer moving about at 11 a.m., it will usually be a buck. Hunt mid-days this fall and test the hypothesis for yourself. I can almost guarantee that you'll be surprised at what you see.

Dealing with Baiters

Using bait while deer hunting is legal in 25 of the 42 states with huntable whitetail populations. Baiting is especially popular in Texas, Michigan and Wisconsin, where hunters literally spend millions of dollars annually on corn, apples, carrots, pumpkins, sugar beets, sweet potatoes and just about anything else deer will eat. I've spent countless hours listening to the "great bait debate," especially since chronic wasting disease was found east of the Mississippi River.

The baiting issue is volatile — you either love it or hate it. There's little middle ground. In fact, I could probably write an entire book on that subject alone. My purpose of bringing it up here is twofold: 1. To acknowledge that it does affect behavior, and 2. To provide tips to nonbaiters who must try to live in harmony with baiting neighbors.

Research by Wisconsin deer biologists indicates that 40 percent of that state's bowhunters and slightly fewer gun-hunters admit to using bait at least some time during the hunting season. The research also indicates that success rates are slightly higher for baiting bowhunters vs. hunters who don't bait. Ironically, the success rate for gun-hunters who bait is substantially lower vs. gun-hunters who do not bait. That difference can be directly linked to the whitetail's uncanny ability to detect human pressure and modify its behavior to deal with it.

All things being equal, baiting is an effective way to kill unpressured deer. However, it is also the best way to alter deer behavior, and that's not a good thing. Pressured deer living near bait piles are extremely tough to hunt. The law of diminishing returns definitely comes into play: Baiters often take one or two adult deer (usually does) during the first week of the season, then find themselves filling out the meat pole with fawns and yearlings. There hasn't been any research on this, but it's my estimation that buck fawn harvests would be higher on baited properties as opposed to unbaited properties. I make that assumption because studies have shown that buck fawns are invariably the first deer to appear at a food source, and I've noticed that the majority of bait-hunters (with the exception of Texas trophy hunters) are nondiscriminatory.

Are baiters evil? Of course not. I have many friends who abide by the rules and enjoy their time in the woods. I have also tried it, and have killed a few deer. Those hunts, however, left hollow feelings in my stomach. Let's just say baiting was not my cup of tea.

Is baiting wrong from a biological standpoint? Yes, most definitely. I have yet to find one professional deer biologist who believes baiting, or supplemental feeding for that matter, is good for the long-term health of any deer herd (again, not including Texas). But I digress. Baiting is here to stay in many states. If nonbaiters want to enjoy maximum time afield, they have to learn how to hunt harder and smarter than their baiting neighbors. Believe me, I'm talking from experience.

Part of a recent hunting season included one of those hard lessons. Our late-November gun season was going to be my wife's first in two years. Tracy was pregnant the previous gun season and gave birth to our daughter the next summer, so she was champing at the bit to get back in the woods. We spent weeks preparing for the hunt – buying extra hand-warmers, socks and even a new pair of pac boots. She absolutely hates cold weather! I also invested $200 in one of those fancy carbon-lined pop-up blinds so we could hunt together at the edge of a large field. Long story short: I paid the neighbors a visit the week before opening day only to realize they were hauling buckets of bait to their stands that were located back in the woods a few hundred yards from Tracy's ground blind. It wasn't illegal, but I immediately knew it would definitely alter how deer used the field we hunted.

WHY INSIDE CORNERS ARE SAFE BETS

✔ Comparatively few hunters have access to thousands, much less hundreds, of acres of prime deer hunting ground. If you're like me, you have a couple of OK spots on marginal land, and you must deal with neighbors, property lines and the like. And, it always seems like the best spot on the property is right on the border of someone else's land. Instead of staring at topo maps and racking your brain in an attempt to find the perfect spot to place your stand, do a quick overview and highlight major terrain features.

Invariably, you'll find the property has at least one inside corner. It could be the back edge of a field where it meets some woods, or it could be a woodland opening that's sandwiched by a creek and possibly an old fence line. Whatever the case, inside corners – any spot where two or more terrain features meet – are great spots for first-time sits when you're unfamiliar with how local deer use the property.

The best inside corners are found when a field is bordered on two sides by thick cover or a large chunk of woodland. The reason is simple: Deer feel more comfortable entering an open area when they have more than one travel option. In the field instance mentioned here, the corner bordered by woods provides just that. In such situations, well-used trails can typically be found in the corner's peak and in select spots very close by. Also, deer often use several parallel trails farther into the woods.

Hunting a field-edge corner can be productive during the early season and closer to the rut, but a better option is to set up inside the woods along trail intersections and, better yet, near parallel trails. Mature bucks often use parallel trails to scent-check fields from afar. When scouting, identify these trails and place stands based solely on wind direction. Finally, don't forget that a little bit of legwork in the off-season will often pay huge dividends when hunting season rolls around.

My inclination was correct. Tracy hunted hard, sitting in that blind for a total of 27 hours during the gun season and the only deer we saw appeared within a few minutes of closing time. In fact, she sat three straight days that week without seeing a single deer. The deer usually grazed in the field, but stopped that activity nearly overnight when they found the new "food sources." The neighbors? They shot at least two deer, and both were taken within minutes of shooting time. Again, they did nothing illegal or even impolite. After all, they were hunting their own land. And, yes, one example does not provide for scientific conclusions. However, I can confidently conclude, based on my experience of observing deer behavior, that the nearby bait piles played a huge role in Tracy's string of poor hunting days.

We lamented about that "lost season" for weeks ... probably months. When our disappointment subsided, we realized we had to revise our plans to make sure it didn't happen again. We eventually settled on hunting a different area with a few revised tactics. That meant hunting thicker cover when faced with nearby baiters and adopting a new approach that saw us arrive in our stands earlier in the morning. These two tactics are ubiquitous for hunting pressured deer in just about any situation. With that in mind, here are four tactics you can use to outsmart a baiter.

1. Hunt thick cover. The best scenario is to hunt staging cover deer use to access baited properties. In other words, you have to intercept them on their way the neighbor's property.

2. Hunt travel corridors. Similarly, hunt spots on your property that deer typically use to access bedding areas. These areas might not even be close to the property lines. However, deer often fall back into traditional travel patterns after they've filled up at a bait station.

3. Key on preferred browse. Just because deer fill up on bait doesn't mean they forget about their favorite foods. In fact, studies in Maine indicate that deer usually overbrowse areas adjacent to long-term bait sites. These browsing areas are often easy to hunt because deer trails become well worn.

4. Step on some toes. If your neighbor impolitely baits near your property lines, alter your entrance and exit routes to your stands so you walk as close to these bait sites as possible while, of course, staying on your property. Your mere presence will contaminate the area with at least some human scent, and deer will adopt new routes to accessing those bait sites. You just might find that the deer will change their patterns so they cross farther into your property during daylight. I never like recommending a tactic that's as caddy as this one, but I fully realize that some people simply cannot be reasoned with. In those instances, I prefer such subtle non-confrontational approaches to dealing with a situation. Such tactics, however, should only be used as an absolute last resort.

Step 3
Think Like A Deer

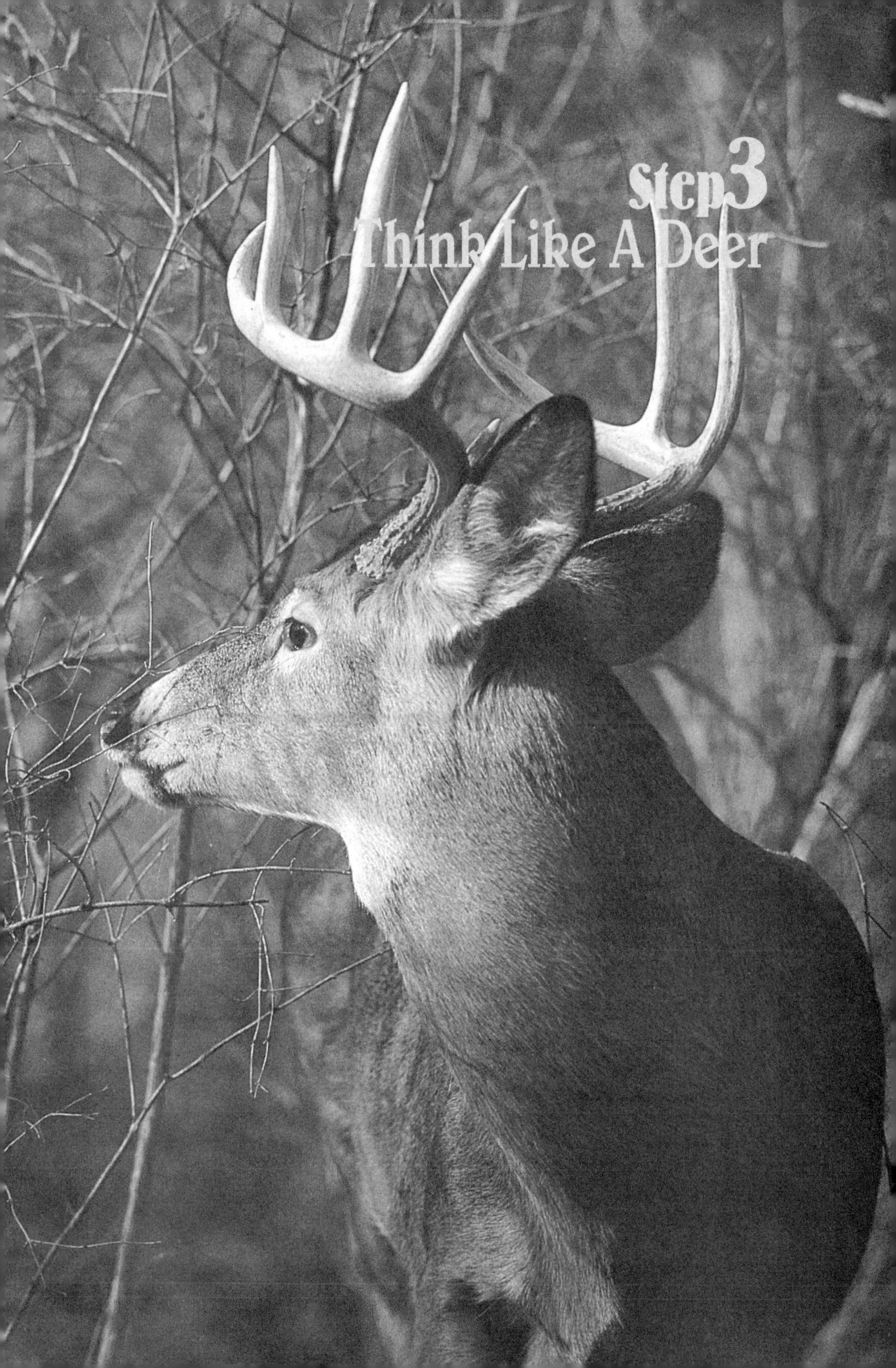

Be careful when using trail cameras. Adopt a scent-free approach and avoid placing cameras in bedding areas. Mature deer will quickly change their patterns if they sense any type of human pressure.

here's a difference between anthropomorphism and common-sense hunting tactics. Of course, the latter is quite the oxymoron. As baseball great Paul Molitor once said, "If common sense were so common, wouldn't everyone have it?" It should also be noted that many great hunters fail miserably when trying to predict deer behavior based on "what should happen." This is highly evident on many blood trails, where deer behavior is highly inconsistent. However, all things equal, hunters can routinely outsmart white-tailed deer by applying a dash of common sense with heaping helpings of patience and persistence.

Know Your Surroundings

There's a fine line between predicting what a deer will do and out-thinking yourself. Today's hunters spend way too much time analyzing maps, plat books and aerial photos trying to guess what deer will do "on paper." These items are great tools to get a starting point for a piece of property, but they do nothing to put a deer on the ground. The only way to truly learn deer behavior and travel patterns is to make a few educated guesses, then get your butt in a tree stand or ground blind and see firsthand how deer use that particular property.

Some basic knowledge of flora and fauna can help a hunter to instant success. Specifically, intimate knowledge of a property's tree, shrub and plant communities can eliminate a lot of the guesswork. If a hunter knows what deer eat and when they'll eat it, he can start thinking like a deer and quicken the learning curve.

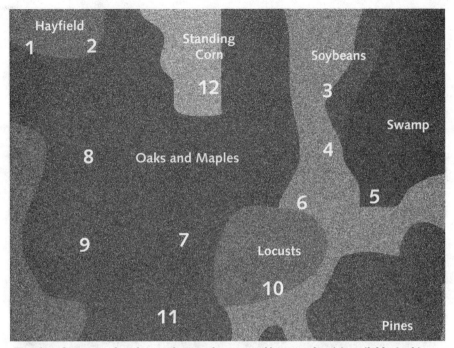

Deer love farm crops, but they prefer succulent natural browse when it's available. In this 150-acre scenario, a hunter could easily maintain a dozen stand sites and hunt them on a rotational basis. That is, the hunter would "follow the food" throughout the season, hunting it during the times of autumn when deer prefer it the most.

There are many defining moments in a deer hunter's career. One of mine came a decade ago when I shared an Alabama deer camp with Dr. Ray McIntyre, a bowhunting legend and former owner of the Warren & Sweat Tree Stand Company. McIntyre, now retired, is a master archer who was killing whitetails with his bow and arrows long before he was in the hunting business. As a credit to his uncanny woodsmanship, and thanks to liberal Southern bag limits, he had bow-killed more than 300 whitetails. As previously mentioned, no hunter can rack up numbers like that without having some prime places to hunt. However, in McIntyre's case, his endless close encounters with whitetails were definitely linked to his ability to read and understand woodland environments.

Deer hunting has changed a lot over the past 20 years, but woodsmanship never goes out of style. McIntyre's many seasons of experience taught him how to instantly identify preferred food sources and instinctively know when and how to hunt them. "Few people fully understand all the favorite early-season food of the whitetail," he said. "Fewer still can identify them. If you can't find them, you can't hunt them."

Talk about a wakeup call. When I met McIntyre, I'm sure I came across as a punk kid who thought he knew all the answers. Needless to say, his words were humbling, because, frankly, I really hadn't a clue on how deer used natural forages throughout autumn. I was certainly one of those hunters who wasted my time by

This Wisconsin buck was killed in a transition area between a young clearcut and a thick creek bottom.

looking for old rubs, scrapes and even shed antlers during March, June, July and August scouting trips. "That information might serve you well during the rut, but it don't mean diddly when you're trying to kill a deer during the early season," McIntyre said.

I spent five days with McIntyre, following him around the woods like a true apprentice. Instead of looking for buck sign, we focused on identifying each plant and tree species. These lessons took place in a true Southern classroom, but what I learned there has paid huge dividends in my home deer haunts of Wisconsin – and every other whitetail location I've hunted ever since. The most important lesson was how deer use oak woodlots. How many times have you walked in the woods, realized acorns were falling and returned to camp proclaiming you've finally located the mother of all deer hunting spots? It happens to all of us. Unfortunately, merely finding acorns isn't enough, unless, of course, your goals are set extremely low. Not all oaks produce acorns annually, and deer prefer some species to others.

Follow Browse Trends

Acorns fall under two basic categories – white and red – with white oak nuts being most preferred by deer because of their lower acid content. It gets a little tricky after that, however, as there are literally dozens of varieties spread across both categories.

Production also varies. Some white-oak strains can produce annual crops, while red oaks need at least two seasons to produce just one crop. That's why it's important to know exactly how many oaks grow in your woods, how productive they are, and what their recent histories for mast production looks like. If you haven't paid attention, merely map out your hunting area and approach future hunts with at least the knowledge of location and current mast conditions. This approach will at least get you started for next year.

Oaks are easy to identify. Reds have pointed leaf fingers, while whites have dull, rounded points. Red varieties include the general red oak and the lesser strains of jack, pin, scarlet, black, blackjack, scrub and turkey oaks. White varieties include the general white oak and the lesser strains of post, bur, swamp, overcup, live, laurel, water, willow, chestnut and chinquapin oaks. Even seasoned veterans have trouble positively identifying all of these species. Therefore, it's wise to invest $20 or so into a tree identification guide like those offered by Houghton & Mifflin.

Mississippi's Will Primos is another master deer hunter whom I admire greatly. In fact, if it wasn't for him, I might have never learned how to key off of locust groves during the early season. Although they're abundant in the South, locusts can also be found in the North. These thorny trees grow tall and produce bushels of banana-shaped pods in autumn. Deer absolutely love locust pods, but don't run out and plant a grove of these trees tomorrow. They're a highly invasive species that will quickly choke out more preferred trees and shrubs. However, if you happen to have a locust grove on your hunting property, you should definitely look at it more closely.

My first taste of deer hunting in a locust grove came in the mid-1990s when I bowhunted with Primos at Mississippi's Tara Wildlife Area. It was early November – weeks before the rut – and deer were bulking up on acorns, wild pecans and nearly every other kind of natural forage. Feeding patterns changed, however, midway through our hunt when honey locust pods started raining from the trees. One afternoon I watched in awe as five yearling bucks approached an ancient tree that was dropping pods by the dozen. The deer tolerated each other's presence while dining on the tasty treats. Locust pods are similar to pea pods in the fact that they contain legume-type fruits. A deer will use its front teeth to pick up a locust pod before positioning it sideways to begin chewing. The deer keeps chewing until all of the fruits pop from the hull. The hull eventually exits the opposite jaw. Watching these deer eat locust pods reminded me of how a ticker tape is dispensed from a machine. The Southern honey locust can grow as tall as 80 feet. Its Northern cousin is the somewhat shorter black locust, which often drops its pods in early autumn.

I didn't capitalize on black locusts until a few years after I hunted with Primos. It was late September, and I was hunting a small private woodlot sandwiched between a winding river and a busy county highway. I obtained hunting permission just four days before the season opener and, therefore, had little time for scouting. My goal was simply to put some venison in the freezer, so I tossed a plat book and my knee-high rubber boots into the bed of my pickup before leaving for work one morning. The plan was to walk the 80-acre parcel and find at least two stand sites for opening weekend. That didn't take long. While skirting the property along the riverbank,

Smart use of deer scents begins and ends with a scent-free hunter.

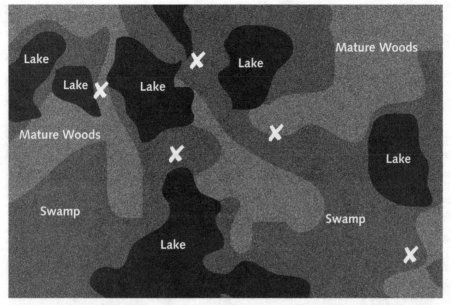

Lake country whitetail hunters should take full advantage of the natural runways created by ponds, drainages and kettle lakes. Deer activity is easily determined in swampy areas, as travel routes become apparent through well-used trails leading from feeding areas to bedding areas. The Xs on this map show five prime stand sites that allow the hunter to take full advantage of the landscape.

I noticed a small ridge that wound toward the north property line. I climbed the ridge and found an old logging road that was lined with mature black locusts – branches drooping from bumper crops of pods. I returned the next afternoon with my climbing stand and high hopes. The hunt didn't last long. Deer literally poured out of the surrounding cover as the sun inched toward the treetops. They headed straight for the locust pods and were soon munching them at a frenzied rate. I had several doe tags in my pocket, so I waited for the largest one to feed her way toward my stand. The shot was true, and she didn't go far. That was probably the most satisfying early season bowhunt I've ever had, because I used newfound knowledge to outsmart a whitetail.

Common Sense About Scents

Scent usage is one of today's hottest topics among serious hunters. Whitetails live and die by their noses, and by the time a buck reaches maturity, his nasal gland has filtered millions – if not trillions – of odors. Is a whitetail's sense of smell as good as it's cracked up to be? I'd say definitely. Scent, or lack of it, probably plays a role in every successful hunt. Some hunters undoubtedly get lucky by guessing right or by catching a deer with its guard down, but consistent success completely hinges upon a hunter's ability to reduce his scent while basing his hunting tactics around thermal currents and prevailing wind directions.

Locusts are an overlooked source of preferred whitetail food.

Thermals are fairly easy to understand. In a nutshell, air currents rise uphill during mornings and filter downhill during evenings. Topographical characteristics do provide for some more wrinkles to those descriptions, but cross currents and the like aren't worth worrying about, because they're simply too unpredictable.

Many outdoor writers like to make up "newfound research" concerning the whitetail's sense of smell. I recently read a piece where the author used another tired anthropomorphic analogy where he compared humans to deer. "A human might walk into a restaurant and smell onions and beer," he wrote. "If a deer walked into the same place, it would smell onions, beer, pickles, mustard, cigar smoke and cheap perfume, and react based on past experiences." Buck pellets! Although the general point might be valid, the analogy is terribly flawed. Deer don't walk through the woods with cognizant thought. They're not ambling around saying to themselves, "Hmm, I smell dog urine in Old Man Johnson's back forty. Guess I best be avoiding that place for a while."

Deer are intelligent animals, but their intelligence is based purely on the instinctual reflexes of a prey species. In other words, they react – most often quickly and decisively – to out-of-place stimuli. It might be an odd odor, flash of white from a T-shirt, or subtle metallic sound from a tree stand. They sense something and skedaddle. They don't stand around analyzing it.

Commercial scent makers have received much criticism over the years because a few shady characters viewed the industry as a way of getting rich by hawking inferior products. As is the case with most businesses, the wannabes have run themselves out of business. Today's market includes some great products that definitely help hunters fool more deer.

White oaks feature leaves with rounded lobes. Unlike the red oak, which can only produce mast every other year, white oaks are capable of producing annual acorn crops.

Although I'm a big fan of commercial deer scents, I limit my usage to the basics: scent-killing soaps and sprays, and – during rut-time hunts – doe-in-estrous urines and synthetic lures. Scents are not magical. They simply provide the hunter with one more tool for outsmarting a deer. Reducing human odor is the No. 1 key to any successful hunt. That's why a serious scent-elimination plan is usually the difference between goodness and greatness. It's even more important when hunting bucks.

My program is simple but rigid. I shower before every hunt, using a commercial product like the Scent Killer liquid soap from Wildlife Research Center. I then dress in nonhunting clothes (usually a long-sleeve T-shirt and sweatpants) and pull on a pair of spare rubber boots that I use just for driving. I sometimes even go so far as to place a clean bed sheet on the seat of my car, because the leather seat is a sure trap for foreign odors. My hunting clothes and boots stay sealed in a zippered Hunters Specialties scent-proof bag until I'm at my hunting area. I usually park by some evergreens or a thick fence line and use them as my "dressing room." This approach might sound over the top. I've had many people laugh at me for "being a weirdo." No skin off my nose. Ever since adopting this program eight years ago, I've seldom been winded by deer while hunting. In fact, I can count those instances on one hand, and in all of the cases, I attribute sloppy preparation on my part as the reason why they smelled me.

I should note that my total-control program coincided with my use of activated-carbon suits. I've used suits from Scent-Lok and Robinson Labs and found both to be very effective in reducing human scent. Admittedly, a recent scientific study concluded that activated-carbon suits didn't do much to hinder the tracking ability of trained dogs. In my opinion, that study was inconclusive, because free-ranging

Successful hunters keep meticulous notes ... even of deer killed by other members of their hunting party.

deer are complete opposites. They do not walk the woods seeking human scent; they react to it. I believe activated-carbon suits greatly diminish the amount of scent that's emitted into the air. I also attribute many of my successful hunts on mature deer to the luxury of wearing a Scent-Lok suit while hunting stands placed upwind of preferred travel corridors.

How Deer Change as They Age

If deer and humans do have one thing in common it's this: Age brings change. Avid hunters often bandy about the word "maturity" when referring to deer they've killed. Maybe we think we're great hunters if we can routinely dupe the kinds of deer that are supposed to give us the slip 99 percent of the time. What is maturity anyway? According to biologists, a whitetail isn't mature until it's 4.5 years old. And, by the way, very few deer can be aged accurately on the hoof, or, in the case of a large buck, by its antlers. Tooth-wear analysis is still the only reliable method for determining a deer's age, except for in Texas, where tooth wear is exaggerated. Texas deer wear down their teeth more rapidly because their diet often includes plants and shrubs grown in gritty soils, etc.

Although they're constantly avoiding pitfalls and predators, buck fawns have it pretty easy. They spend the first six months of their lives following Mom around while learning the intricacies of the natural word. Life becomes a bit more difficult when a buck enters his second summer and officially enters yearling status. By now, he's likely to have dispersed 1 to 20 miles from his birthing site, and he's pretty much on his own. Throughout this summer he'll roam with other males from his age class, eating, growing and learning new territory. He'll be a brand-new animal when August gives way to September, as he'll shed his velvet and sport his first polished rack – be it spikes, forks or a small basket rack. Meanwhile, yearling does, unless they have a single fawn in tow, will likely be traveling with their mothers, sisters, aunts and even grandmothers.

Fawns are the easiest deer to kill, but not for the obvious reason. They're easiest because they typically represent the age class with the most members. All things being equal, a yearling buck is often easier to kill, especially during early archery seasons. I make this blanket statement based on the fact that yearlings are constantly on the move and often traveling through new territory. Their sense of curiosity rivals that of the common house cat – almost to the point of where they bumble underneath a hunter's tree stand for the mere purpose of checking it out. They're definitely not stupid; they're just a little careless.

There is quite a difference between a 2.5-year-old buck and a 3.5-year-old buck. The 2.5-year-old buck is on his way to becoming a wily creature, but he still has lapses in judgment, so to speak, and still makes some mistakes. The 3.5-year-old buck, on the other hand, is nearing the top of his game. He makes few mistakes, and usually blows out of an area at the slightest intrusion.

Two bucks I killed while bowhunting near my home in recent years make for good examples of these age classes. The first buck was a 2.5-year-old that I arrowed during the early bow season. I hung my stand at the edge of a hayfield that borders

Instead of wasting time analyzing maps, go hunting and make mental notes of everything you see to and from your stand sites.

a large pine forest. It was a warm afternoon, with temperatures peaking in the mid 60s. Realizing I had better be careful with my scent, I dressed in two layers of Scent-Lok, wore clean rubber boots and carried a bottle of Carbon Blast scent-killing spray. When I was about 75 yards from my stand, I stopped and again thoroughly sprayed my boots, pant legs and equipment. The afternoon wore on without a single deer sighting. However, just as evening approached, the buck appeared in the woods and walked a trail leading straight for the field edge and my stand. He stopped and stood to test the wind once or twice, but he wasn't ultra-cautious. When he reached the base of my tree, he again stopped and tested the wind. Amazingly, he noticed the wet rungs of my ladder and proceeded to lick them … unaware that a predator was 20 feet up that tree. The buck finally broke for the field edge, and I sent an arrow through both of his lungs.

Fast-forward three years. Same spot. Same time of year. Nearly the same tree. I am again hunting the early season, and, in a near repeat performance, a buck appears just before sunset. However, this high-tined 8-pointer is a 3.5-year-old, and he's a lot smarter than his cousin from a few years ago. The buck appears 50 yards behind my stand, and I'm alerted to his presence when he snorts/coughs twice. I turn slowly to see the buck with his nose in the air, swirling it ever so slowly in an attempt to pinpoint the odor he has detected. The buck continues this investigation for precisely 17 minutes (yes, I timed it!). Fortunately for me, the buck is just on the outside of my scent stream. The light breeze is out of the west, and he's standing southeast of my stand. Still, the buck senses something and eventually turns and walks back to the safety of the pine grove

The 3.5-year-old buck gave me the slip, but he didn't have an error-free day. An hour later, with just 15 minutes of shooting time remaining, the buck reappeared and slowly worked a trail toward the field. He stopped many times to test the wind, and he even worked a licking branch and then thrashed a small pine tree. It was a classic example of how a mature buck uses a field-side staging area. He was going to hang back in the woods until last light ... then enter the field. Thankfully for me, I had hung that stand 50 yards inside the woods for that very reason. After several excruciating moments, the buck stepped within 18 yards. I drew my bow, bleated with my voice to get him to stop, and sent an arrow through his heart. After the shot, I slumped back into my stand and realized I had quite the tension headache. Unlike the hunt for the 2.5-year-old buck, this slightly older buck had refined his senses so well that I knew I would have never killed him had I not done everything by the book.

Do Mature Bucks Have Memories?

Although I've previously mentioned that I don't believe animals possess rational thought, I do believe deer possess some type of memory mechanism. Granted, this statement is made from many personal observations, but it seems plausible – even if only Pavlovian in nature – that a wild whitetail can encounter enough repeat experiences to "learn" how to react to certain stimuli. I do not believe deer possess long-term memories, but I'd venture a guess that instincts allow them to be conditioned to avoid perceived danger areas for perhaps half of a hunting season.

A good example of this point occurred when I was bowhunting in southern Illinois about 10 years ago with Jerry Petersen and Gary Sefton of Woods Wise Products. I was perched 20 feet up a red oak when an enormous 10-pointer appeared on a nearby ridge and walked straight for my tree. The buck stopped and quartered away when he was 35 yards out. Hands shaking, I drew my bowstring, aimed high on his chest and released the arrow. It sailed a foot over his back. The buck whirled and bolted back up the ridge.

Three hours later, a doe appeared and sprinted to the base of my tree. Panting hard, she stopped and looked back over her shoulder. Sure enough, the same 10-pointer was in tow. The buck approached cautiously, then stopped when he was about 50 yards out. Despite having a hot doe in front of him, the buck wouldn't budge. He stood motionless for a few moments before whirling and bolting back up the ridge. True, he could have smelled me, or possibly the arrow that lay 15 yards in front of him, but based on his actions, I believe he remembered something wasn't right about that particular spot in the woods. If it were memory, it was most likely short term, which brings me to my point: long-term memory.

Over the years, I've visited many hunting camps that get pounded with hunting pressure. The best example was an Alabama lodge that hosted about a dozen hunters per week for more than three months each fall. This camp included about 9,500 acres of hunting land, but the outfitter only had about 25 tree stands in place. Hunters were not allowed to hang their own stands and, therefore, had to "go 'round the mulberry bush" as one of the guides put it. In other words, some of the stands were hunted every morning and afternoon for weeks on end. I sat in several such stands

YOUNG BUCKS USUALLY FIND NEW ZIP CODES

❦ Dispersal of young bucks is perhaps one of the most poorly misunderstood aspects of deer biology among hunters. Dispersal is highly complex because it hinges on many factors, including the health of the deer herd, population dynamics, food availability and region of the country. What most hunters do not realize – or stubbornly fail to admit – is that the young buck they see this year will likely be nowhere to be found next year. I should preface that by noting that this discussion only applies if your hunting area is 1 contiguous square mile (640 acres) or less.

In a recent survey of *Deer & Deer Hunting* readers, I asked, "If a hunter is hunting a 640-acre parcel (1 square mile) this fall and sees a button buck, what are the chances the hunter will see that same buck on the same property next year (if the buck survives)?" Nearly 25 percent of these high-end deer hunters thought there was an 80 percent chance of seeing the buck, and 66 percent said they thought there was a 50 percent chance.

Although there is no concrete answer for the hypothetical question, the odds of seeing that buck fawn are more like 0 percent to 20 percent. More than 1000 *D&DH* readers took a stab at that question, and only 65 got it right. That goes to show that despite everything we've learned over the past 30 years, science is still teaching us lessons about the white-tailed deer. According to scores of scientific research projects, the most recent being conducted in western New York, it has been proven highly unlikely for a buck fawn to inhabit the same square mile of habitat when it turns 1 year old and grows its first set of antlers. Fawns typically, but not always, disperse in spring. Big-woods fawns disperse when they're yearlings in autumn. Dispersal distances vary, but fawns generally relocate 1 to 35 miles from where they were born *(see Chapter 8 for more on this discussion)*.

Despite their tendency to roam far and wide, young bucks can withstand hunting losses without affecting the so-called quality of a deer herd. Deer densities across the United States vary from 5 deer per square mile to 100 dpsm, with the average falling somewhere between 35 and 50, depending on region. Many factors come into play when determining harvest strategies, but, generally speaking, a square-mile of habitat in the 50 dpsm range can withstand a buck-fawn harvest of three animals without compromising management goals. The main point: Don't be so paranoid about killing antlerless deer that you worry needlessly about killing buck fawns.

"When I hear that (myth), it just irks me, because it's totally way off," legendary whitetail hunter Brad Harris once told me. "Every situation is different. You have to match your calling with the terrain and conditions."

Some hunters have also claimed that deer can readily decipher tones and determine which calls come from bucks and which ones come from does. Again, that's pure nonsense. With the exception of fawn bleats, deer cannot use sounds alone to identify strangers in their midst. "A buck doesn't have the capacity to hear a sound and then think to himself, 'Oh, that was a yearling buck,' or 'That was a 3-year-old buck.' He needs to see the other deer," Harris added. A doe's grunt is usually lower in pitch than a buck's, but not always.

A fourth myth involves when to stop calling. Many seasoned hunters claim that you should always stop calling once you have a deer's attention. As evidenced in the aforementioned hunt, that's a big mistake. Deer are good listeners, not great ones. "You have to back up that first call with another one if the buck hasn't committed to coming your way," Harris said. "I can't count the number of deer that I've killed by following up with a call once I've gotten their attention. That follow-up call is often the difference between a close encounter and one that puts the deer in shooting range."

Finally, some hunters and outdoor writers have stated that deer calling is a tactic any average hunter can use all season to dupe wary whitetails. If that's the case, I'm a well-below-average deer hunter. Making the sounds might be easy enough, but it takes an extremely skilled hunter to dupe pressured whitetails during the early and late seasons. Calling requires common sense and a realistic approach. Use aggressive tactics during the rut, and save the subtle tactics for the pre- and post-rut periods.

Step 4
Play Above The Competition

Mature deer quickly adapt and change their travel patterns after opening weekend of hunting season.

The tiny flashlight beam darted back and forth across the swamp like a water bug in a rain puddle. I sighed out loud, clenched my teeth and muttered something not fit for print. It was a neighboring hunter, and he was headed toward his deer stand at first light. Although I was nearly certain he had ruined my morning – one that saw me awake at 3:30 a.m. to make the long drive to this hunting spot. After losing his way, the hunter finally found his stand and banged his way up the tree with an old steel climber. From the sound of it, he was only 100 yards from my stand.

"Got to be patient," I told myself. Well, I was patient, and it didn't pay off. I had vowed to hunt until noon, but that plan changed when the hunter called it quits at 9 a.m., clanked his way back down the tree and spooked a buck and three does that were headed my way. Despite the blown opportunities, I learned how to outsmart something more than a deer that morning. It took a few more similar episodes, but I learned that the other hunter only hunted Saturday mornings during the archery season. Later that season, I put in my vacation slip and headed to my stand early on a Wednesday morning. The woods were quiet, and what I believe were the same four deer appeared at nearly the same time on the same trail. That buck's antlers might have never made it to my office wall had I continued battling the weekend warrior. The key to that hunt? Those deer were extremely sensitive to human pressure. By changing hunting tactics, I was able outsmart the deer and the other persistent hunter.

To consistently bag deer, you need to know where the bedding areas are and what seasonal foods deer prefer. For example, berry and red-maple browse are early season whitetail magnets.

Hunting Pressured Deer

High expectations run rampant among today's hunters. In fact, it's probably the No. 1 topic I run across on a daily basis working at *Deer & Deer Hunting*. North America's antler craze is officially in high gear, and there really isn't an end in sight. That's not necessarily a bad thing. After all, we all thrill at the sight of a mature buck – but it borders on an unhealthy obsession when we let it cloud reality. Hunters who hunt pressured deer – be it on public land or small, overcrowded private parcels – often find themselves (usually knowingly) in the latter category because they simply expect too much from the hunting experience.

No hunter in North America, especially the so-called celebrities, could regularly kill mature deer from most of the properties that most of us hunt. They might have a few extra tricks up their collective sleeve, but trust me, most of these guys are merely blessed to have access to great land and unpressured deer.

What's the definition of pressure? That's a hard one. For simplicity's sake, let's approach the answer from a hunter-density standpoint. To hunt mature deer, you really shouldn't be hunting more than two guys per 80 acres of high-quality land. Even then, you have to pick and choose your spots. Pound it too hard, and you'll send those deer on high alert in a hurry. Where does that leave the guy who hunts public land? Well, you probably get the idea. That's why adopting a nontraditional game plan is the best tactic for hunting pressured properties. The following five tactics will help you outsmart other hunters and wrap your tags around more deer … deer that you might have otherwise thought didn't exist.

1. Sign up for an off-peak plan. Face it, most guys are weekend warriors. I don't use that term in a derogatory sense; it merely depicts how most folks approach hunting. They get a few weeks of vacation each year and usually wrap hunts around holiday weekends and the occasional Friday afternoon. There's nothing wrong with that, except for the fact that deer quickly adapt and change their travel patterns after opening weekend of hunting season.

The savvy hunter takes advantage of such human behavior before even thinking about how to outsmart a whitetail. It might be awfully inconvenient and mess up your schedule, but consider taking your time off during the middle of the week to hunt. I recently reviewed my yearly hunting logs and noticed that I've taken a lot of deer on Tuesdays. It certainly could be a coincidence, but I do recall that I've usually had the woods to myself during such off times.

2. Find odd spots. They don't necessarily have to be miles off the beaten path or on the opposite side of a huge lake. In fact, some of the best public deer hunting spots are those little pieces of state and county land that allow hunting near fishing access areas. For example, a little 20-acre chunk of stream access might be all you need to waylay a buck during the early archery season. Scout these areas while turkey hunting and note deer trails and crossings. Pick out a few trees that will be suitable for a climbing tree stand and then revisit the area during an off-peak hunting time in fall. Mid-week mornings are best, but afternoon hunts can be productive. The only problem with afternoon hunts is your chances of interference increase as other guys get out of work and decide to sit the last hour or so of shooting light.

3. Be an early bird. Nothing discourages a public-land hunter like the sight of another pickup truck in "his" parking spot. Consistently successful hunters arrive early and stay late. In heavily hunted areas, early might mean getting to your tree a full hour to 90 minutes before shooting light. This is a tough way to hunt, especially when it's cold, but it works. Conscientious hunters invariably drive away and hunt another spot, rather than risk ruining two hunts by barging in on someone who's already strapped in and waiting for daylight. While we're on the topic, be courteous. Don't think that just because it's public land you have the right to trample past a guy who's already there and bang your stand up a tree 50 yards from him. Treat others the way you'd want to be treated. It makes for better hunting in the long run, anyway, because they might be more inclined to return the favor if you beat them out there next time.

4. Don't broadcast your spots. I seldom park near areas I'll be hunting. In fact, I usually go way out of my way to disguise my entry and exit routes. This is especially true for public-land hunts, but it also applies to private land areas that I have all to myself. The more I broadcast where I'll be hunting, the more likely I am to have someone barge in on me when hunting public land, or have a jealous neighbor fire up his chainsaw at prime time when the sun's dipping below the treetops. This tactic has saved my hunts many times. Granted, it can be a double-edged sword when hunting public land, especially during firearms seasons because others might think they have the woods to themselves. That's why I always tie orange ribbons near my tree stand, or hang an extra orange vest nearby, when gun-hunting on public land.

Filling doe tags early will provide meat for the freezer and provide for more enjoyable buck-hunting as autumn progresses.

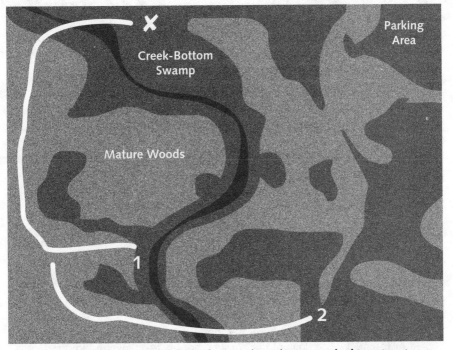

No matter how hard a property is hunted, strategic tactics are required to outmart wary whitetails. This is especially true during gun seasons when less-serious hunters use the same routes to their stands. In this scenario, the hunter bypasses the easy routes and skirts the property to enter his stands. This tactic allows the hunter to take advantage of surrounding pressure, and allows him to keep more deer on his property.

5. Work hard after a kill. Like tactic No. 4, it's not wise to drag a deer out of the woods for all to see. It might require a lot of extra work, but avoid dragging a deer down a well-used walking trail, snowmobile route or logging road. If you must use those routes, invest in a sled or a rickshaw-type cart. Wrap your deer in a tarp to avoid leaving bloodstains behind. You definitely want to celebrate your success back at camp, but not out in the woods for all to see. My hunting partners and I learned this lesson the hard way; otherwise "secret" public-land spots were soon invaded by other hunters when they saw us dragging deer out of the woods at midday.

Staying Tough When It's Late

In many ways, deer hunting is a lot like long-distance running: The most successful participants are those who invest the time and a never-say-die attitude. That's why adopting a precise late-season hunting plan is one of the best ways to play above the competition. Late-season whitetail hunting is often a lesson in humility. Big bucks all but vanish, and does, fawns and young bucks seemingly know which trails will lead them exactly 10 yards beyond shooting range. Such is the life of a diehard bowhunter. When you start taking things for granted, Mother Nature quickly deals you a sobering hand.

HOW TO PLAY ABOVE THE COMPETITION

❦ **Hunt odd times and odd hours.** We all love to be in our stands at first light, especially when the various seasons kick off. To play above the competition, you need to think outside that box and find spots that put deer in front of you during the very productive midday hours.

❦ **Devise a smart game plan.** Pressured deer are tough to hunt, and you don't stand much of a chance if you play your hand to other hunters. The hunter who keeps his spots secret and hunts them only when other hunters won't be around is the guy who will taste success most often.

❦ **Have varied game plans.** Devise separate hunting strategies for the early season and the late season, and stick to them. It's a given that other hunters will eventually find some of your hotspots. To succeed, you need to always have an ace in the hole. It's equally important to always be on the lookout for that extra backup spot. You'll never know when you need it.

❦ **Dress for success.** Whether it's the brutal cold of the late season or the sticky hot days of the early archery season, assemble hunting outfits that will keep you on stand longer. The old adage, "You can't tag a buck from your living room sofa," is one that all serious deer hunters should heed when shopping for the right gear.

❦ **Get serious during the late season.** A never-say-die attitude is usually the only thing separating the highly successful hunters from the ones who end up with unfilled tags. Late-season hunting isn't easy; it takes some knowledge of deer behavior and patterns and a lot of persistence. Devise a sound game plan and stick with it, especially when the weather gets nasty.

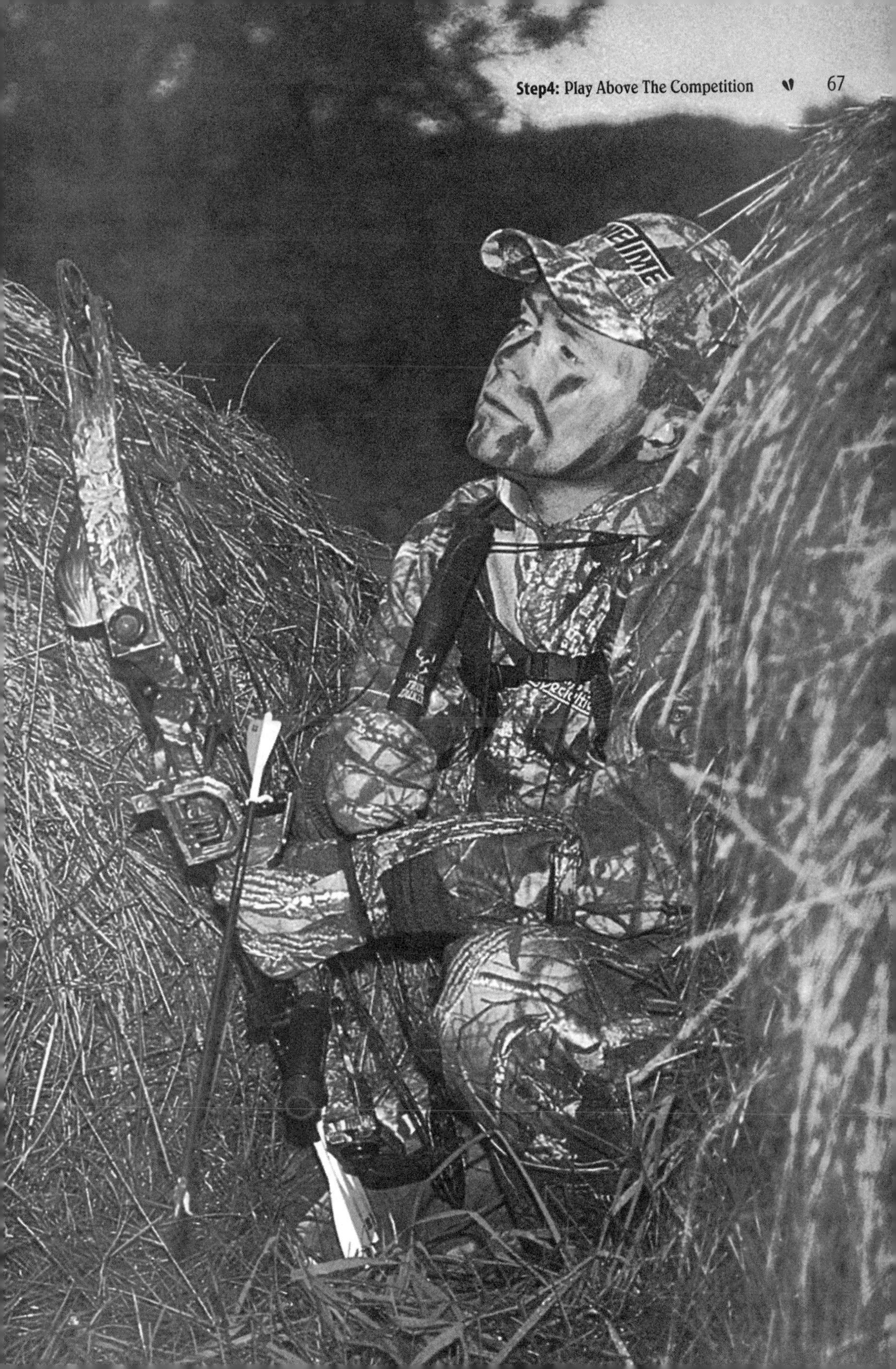

Early season stand sites are usually terrible by the time the late season rolls around. Therefore, take the time to find travel corridors deer use during the fringe hours of daylight.

Although I believe farmland deer are much easier to hunt than their Northern Forest cousins, hunting them requires basically the same approach. Unfortunately, it has taken me weeks, months – and sometimes several seasons – of late-season hunting to truly unravel how deer use a piece of private or public land after mast crops all but disappear in November. Whenever people ask me how they should approach late-season bowhunts, I counter by telling them what they shouldn't do – based on all of the mistakes I have made over the years. The following is a short list of seven common late-season tactics.

1. Don't count on early season stands. It is amazing how much changes in the deer woods in the eight weeks from opening day to the waning rut. Mature does acquire their grayish-blue coats, fawns pack on the weight and bucks become blocky, yet chiseled. There is good reasons for all of those things, and a lot of it has to do with the acorns, soybeans, corn, alfalfa and new-growth browse they were eating not that far from the stands you hung for the mosquito-filled evenings of late September.

It is awfully easy to leave those stands in place and run to them on weekends and the few spare hours we might find on a rare afternoon off in the late season. Huge mistake. No matter what size parcel you are hunting, late-season deer routes are often much different than those of the early season. Take the time to find travel corridors deer use during the fringe hours of daylight. Brushy fence lines, overgrown pastures and bottlenecks in tamarack swamps are good places to start looking for stand locations. Cover is the key, especially after gun season. Deer move during daylight, but most of that movement will be in areas where they feel safe.

2. Don't let your guard down. Late season means cold weather, especially in the North Woods. It is tempting not to shower before hunting when temperatures drop

The virtues of patience and persistence are critical for any type of deer hunting success.

into the 20s and lower. Scent control, however, is even more important now than it is during the early season, because deer have been pressured for weeks.

Use scent-killing soap and shampoo and thoroughly dry off, especially your hair, before heading out for the hunt. Even a hint of moisture will carry some human scent. Place your hunting clothes in a scent-free bag or plastic box, and don't dress until you're at your hunting area. I'll admit this approach isn't always feasible. In those events, I take a bed sheet that I've washed in scent-free soap and drape it over the seat of my car. I will not, however, put on my boots until I'm ready to walk to the woods. I keep them in a Rubbermaid container in the trunk of my car. Before heading out, I spray my boots and pants cuffs with liberal amounts of scent-killing spray. I also brush my teeth with a baking-soda-based toothpaste and pack an apple for a snack, which helps mask breath odor.

3. Be aware of aluminum. My favorite quick ladders, hang-ons and ladder stands are made of welded aluminum, but I seldom use them when hunting in late November and December. Aluminum stands invariably pop, squeak and make other deer-spooking noises when I shift my burly frame during cold-weather hunts. That's why I opt for steel. Many manufacturers offer quality steel steps, ladders and stands. The best ones secure to the tree with a chain, and they are whisper quiet when cinched tight. This isn't to say all aluminum is bad. In fact, stands made from one-piece cast aluminum designs are deathly quiet. So too are stands made of carbon and other composite materials.

LAYER YOUR WAY TO LONGER DAYS AFIELD

You can buy the fastest bow and sharpest broadheads or flattest shooting rifle and best cartridges, but they won't keep you in the deer woods on nasty days. To stay on stand and be in position to shoot that buck of your dreams, you need quality clothing. Don't let anyone fool you. Despite advanced technology, brutal weather still requires serious clothing. And, if you're a big-woods hunter, you'll want the good stuff. Where to look? Good clothing isn't cheap, so it's wise to compare the new products with the tried and true clothing. Compare similar styles; then decide which garments fit your hunting needs.

Layering is still the key to warmth and comfort. Today's high-tech garments do both jobs, but the key is to find garments that come off and go on easily. First and foremost, forget about cotton; it retains moisture and renders all other garments useless when you wear it next to your skin. So, leave those cotton socks, underwear and sweatshirts back at camp. The best first layer will consist of polyester, polypropylene, or something similar. Zyflex is one of my favorite "new" fabrics. It contains microfibers of nylon and Spandex. I have a Zyflex shirt that really keeps my torso warm. It goes on tight, fitting like a rubber glove, but it wicks perspiration away from my body, which allows me to wear fewer layers.

The second layer should consist of something super warm like wool or fleece. I prefer fleece in temperatures ranging from 15 to 30 degrees and wool for anything colder than that. Goose-down liners, insulated bibs and Windstopper garments are great picks for the third layer. Because I bowhunt more than I gun-hunt, my outer garments typically consist of a ScentLok jacket and pants. The Heater Body Suit (www.heaterbodysuit.com) is another option. You can literally wear just one or two layers then crawl into the suit and stay warm all day in sub-zero temperatures. It's definitely worth checking out if you routinely hunt in frigid conditions.

For most of us, price is a factor when selecting clothing. Don't let it cloud your judgment! You will be sorry if go the cheap route when buying cold-weather clothing. Quality costs more, but in the long run, buying top-of-the-line is a wise investment.

To play above the competition, you need to think outside that box and find spots that put deer in front of you during the very productive midday hours.

4. Don't hang stands based solely on map features. It doesn't work. Not for me, anyway. Deer are North America's greatest game animal because they're so unpredictable. We kid ourselves when we walk into the woods and place stands based on areas that merely look good on a topographical map. This approach might get you in the ballpark, but it seldom pinpoints true deer hotspots. For consistent late-season success, you need to know where the bedding areas are and what foods deer are keying on. Don't worry if deer aren't bedding on the property you are hunting. Your property might be a travel corridor from the neighbor's pine plantation to the nearby farmer's picked cornfield. You'll put yourself in position for a shot by knowing the exact trails they use to get from Point A to Point B.

5. Avoid hunting field edges. Field edges are great for seeing deer up close in September, but they're often terrible for hunting in the late season. If you are after big bucks, forget about field edges altogether unless you have secluded fields. Field-edge hunting in late season is usually an afternoon affair, and adult bucks usually enter fields at the cusp of darkness. If you simply want to fill a tag, place your stand inside the woods' edge in some cover. Such patches are often called staging areas, which are places where deer congregate before entering a field. I've used this tactic to kill several deer. Adult does are among the wisest deer in the woods, and they often stand in these small patches of cover to survey a field before entering it. After deciding the coast is clear, they typically trot out of the cover and into the field without hesitating. Field-edge stands are usually unproductive for that reason – deer seldom pause long enough to give you a shot opportunity.

Windy conditions are the exception to this rule. A common myth about big bucks is that they always head for the thickest, nastiest cover when the pressure is on. That's not always true, and, in fact, is sometimes completely false. Anyone who has hunted pressured deer long enough quickly realizes that big bucks often head for open areas on windy days. Wind speeds of 15 mph or more seemingly put deer on edge because they can't pinpoint where danger is coming from.

6. Learn how to dress for success. Staying warm and shooting a bow accurately do not go hand in hand. The bulky clothing you wore for gun season might be prohibitive to making a shot while twisting around the base of a tree. Jacket collars, cuffs and bulky sleeves can easily get in the way of the bowstring. The best approach is to invest in high-tech underwear. This stuff is lightweight, yet keeps you warm on the coldest days. Outer layers should include pants and jacket that are insulated yet streamlined. A knit hat and quality pair of pack boots will also keep you warm where you need it most.

It's wise to check out the Heater Body Suit from T.S.S. Equipment of Cleveland, Wis. The suit is almost like a custom-built sleeping bag. It has saved many of my late-season bowhunts because it allows me to dress very lightly. The suit includes a zipper that opens easily when it is time to stand and shoot. Air-activated hand-warmers are also effective. I use them in my boots, pockets and hand-warming muff. When temperatures drop really low, I wear a kidney belt that accommodates three hand-warmers. Never place hand-warmers near your skin, and don't use them if you have poor circulation. Whichever outfit you wear, be sure to dress in your late-

SEEK PINCH POINTS TO INTERCEPT WARY BUCKS

❦ Most guys simply don't have enough time to scout public-land spots, and that's why they fall into the same trap of hunting areas that look good on topographical maps and the well-beaten trails of nighttime deer routes. You can play above the competition by hunting transition areas leading to these "cow paths."

For example, say you're hunting a swampy creek bottom that borders pines and hardwoods. The creek bottom will surely be littered with deer trails, rubs and scrapes. This great cover is awfully inviting, especially when it also holds a few trees suitable for a climbing tree stand. Although such spots might be great places to hunt in the middle of the week – when other hunters are still grinding it out at work – it's best to seek subtle funnels in the nearby cover. One of the best public-land spots I've hunted consisted of that type of terrain. An 80-acre pine plantation gave way to a creek bottom, which led to a huge hardwood ridge. My buddy and I spent a half-day dissecting the area and discovered three pinch points where the adjacent woodlots necked down into the swamp. These pinch points did not include any heavy deer trails – only faint ones – but they were good enough transition areas to warrant hunting consideration. We each picked a spot and shot deer during our first sit.

The key? The pinch points were areas where the creek, which was knee-deep in most spots, slowed to a trickle. Bucks obviously used these areas as crossings when pressured. That's an important point to keep in mind when hunting pressured deer. While does, fawns and young bucks often use common "fire escapes" to flee pressure, older bucks typically skirt the major trails and slip out of sight by using the lesser-used routes. Such subtle trails aren't always in the most remote reaches of a given property. In fact, both pinch points we found in the aforementioned example were both within 200 yards of a major county road.

Pressured deer are tough to hunt, and you don't stand much of a chance if you play your hand to other hunters.

season outfit and practice shooting from a tree stand. Achieving consistent groups while wearing winter clothing is a lot more difficult than you might think.

7. Don't give up too early. The virtues of patience and persistence are important for any type of deer hunting success, but for late-season success, you need to tattoo them on your psyche. Hunters who leave their stands early are the ones who usually go home with unfilled tags. To taste success, you need to stay to the bitter end on every hunt. What many hunters don't realize is the deer they spook today will be a deer they probably won't see tomorrow. Therefore, you need to always be thinking of the future. For example, if a deer shows up after legal shooting hours, stay in your stand and wait until it leaves or at least moves far enough away so you don't spook it leaving your stand. Busting a deer when you are on the ground isn't nearly as bad as having one see you in your stand.

One of the most exciting times to bowhunt whitetails is when November gives way to December and the throngs of orange-clad gun-hunters have left the woods. It can also be one of the most frustrating. Success can be had, however, by the hunter who spends extra hours afield studying deer behavior and adjusting his tactics accordingly.

Step 5
Simplify Your Approach

If your hunt isn't going to last more than a few hours, reduce clutter by leaving your backpack at home and stuffing the bare essentials into your jacket's cargo pockets.

uccess in any of life's endeavors is usually reserved for those who are organized, motivated and well prepared. It's a simple recipe, and it certainly holds true in deer hunting. How many consistently successful deer hunters do you know? How many of them rely on pure luck? I'll bet none of them are!

To jump on the whitetail wisdom fast track, you need to take what you already know and boil it down to the basics. You don't need outstanding shooting skills, a ton of high-tech gear, or a doctorate in biology. What you do need is a basic understanding of deer behavior, a lot of persistence and determination, and a simple approach. It's the uncomplicated approach that sets the really good hunters apart from the guys who seemingly struggle year in and year out. A clutter-free approach not only speeds up the learning curve, it makes hunting a whole lot more enjoyable.

Scrap that Backpack!

Do you really need to drag along all that extra gear into the woods? Yeah, it's fun to have all those gadgets and gizmos, but how often do you really use them? About the only time I carry a backpack is when I'm hunting out of state and know I'll be in the woods from dark to dark. At home, my tree-stand vigils are seldom longer than five hours. In these instances, I carry a small fanny pack or, more often than not, nothing but my bow. That's why they invented cargo pockets!

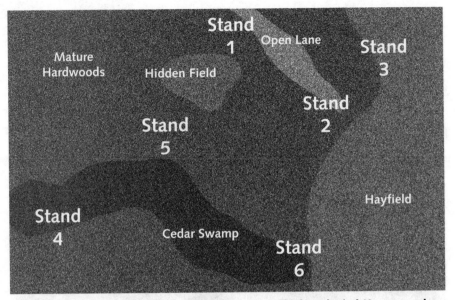

Even small properties can hold many stand-site options. This hypothetical 40-acre parcel holds at least six prime stand sites. Stands 1, 2, 3 and 6, which are near food sources, are ideal for early season hunts. Stands 4 and 5 are good spots for rut-time action because cruising bucks prefer to hold tight to staging cover.

The best way to reduce clutter is to clear your mind by streamlining your approach. If you're hunting a spot that you've already prepped in the pre-season, you should be able to get by with the basics: a knife, small flashlight, bow/gun pull-up rope, grunt call, safety belt tree-attachment assembly, cell phone or two-way radio, and an extra release (if you use one) or cartridges. It's also wise to carry a spray bottle of Scent Killer and a wind puffer or container of wind floaters. These items can be carried in your pockets. Shove a bottle of water in your jacket, along with some jerky or granola bars, and you're ready to rock. I don't always carry my rangefinder when bowhunting, because I learn the shooting distances during pre-season stand preparations. However, I always carry it when gun-hunting, along with a small pair of binoculars. Binoculars are handy for watching deer in the distance, but are most valuable after the shot. I've used mine on several occasions to make mental notes of various landmarks deer ran past as they fled the hit scene. The rangefinder is really handy when gun-hunting, because it allows me not only to know the exact distance of the shot, it helps pinpoint blood trails.

A mature doe I shot a few years ago provides a prime example of how to use a rangefinder to locate blood sign. I was hunting an alfalfa field, and the doe stepped out of the woods within 10 minutes of closing time. I quickly dug my rangefinder out of my jacket and lasered her as she nibbled her way into the field. A push of a button told me she was precisely 143 yards away. I noted how she was standing atop a small rise in the field before leveling my shotgun scope's crosshairs on her shoulder blade. The doe mule-kicked at the shot, whirled and bounded back into

Don't let the sight of one big rub cloud your thoughts on stand placement. Rubs in wide-open areas are usually made at night.

the forest. I immediately knew my slug missed her scapula, but I was confident of a fatal shot nonetheless. Instead of blundering into the woods, I calmly descended my stand and walked toward the rise where she was standing. I then turned around and walked backward, using my rangefinder to measure the distance between the field and the stand until I was 143 yards away. Talk about precise. By now, darkness was settling across the landscape. I pulled out my flashlight, pointed it toward my boots and found blood. Thankfully, the trail was short; the bullet hit the doe through both lungs, and she ran just 100 yards before piling up. Still, it would have taken some time to locate blood in that field had I done it the old-fashioned way.

I've adopted an overall clutter-free hunting approach several years ago and found it led to much more enjoyable hunting. In fact, the only time I really take my fanny pack with me is when I'm hunting a spot that requires an extensive walk. Otherwise, I leave my fanny pack back at my vehicle ... to be retrieved on those special days when I do indeed kill a deer.

Between writing these last few paragraphs, I tramped down to my basement and opened up my fanny pack, spilling all of the contents onto the floor. Here's what was inside: three packs of field-dressing gloves, a roll of biodegradable toilet paper (for marking blood trails), a roll of blaze-orange flagging tape; headlamp-style flashlight; medium-sized handheld flashlight; 12-pack of AA batteries; fillet knife for specific field-dressing chores (reaming); Browning oversized gut-hook tool; vacuum-sealed bag containing matches, a butane lighter and three wafer-thin pieces of cedar kindling;

dragging rope; bubble-style compass and a military-style compass. Rounding out the contents are air-activated hand-warmers, a knit hat and an extra pair of warm gloves. During the hunting season, I also pack an extra bottle of water and a vacuum-sealed bag containing high-energy foods like cashews and granola bars. As you can see, this could easily be called my "blood-trailing survival pack."

How Many Stand Sites?

Reducing stress goes far beyond what gear you should carry afield. A stressful approach especially applies to stand locations. It might seem that having a lot of stand sites on one property would clutter up one's hunting approach. However, the opposite is true. Having many stand options reduces clutter – mind clutter, that is – because it reduces stress by allowing you to worry less about wind conditions, deer feeding patterns and potential interference from other hunters.

How many stand sites are enough, and where should they be located? For starters, to consistently outsmart whitetails, you need to first learn the lay of your hunting property. Ask any turkey hunter, and they'll tell you this is their No. 1 key to success. The same goes for white-tailed deer. That doesn't mean you have to spend every spare minute in the woods looking for every possible ambush location. In fact, as explained in Step 2, I believe it's better to approach unfamiliar properties with a rather conservative approach. Learn the basic terrain features, make a few educated guesses on stand locations, and then hunt the property to learn how deer use it. Too many hunters waste time overanalyzing properties they've seldom hunted. Such strategizing might be fun for some guys, but for me, it's tedious, boring and gets me all stressed out. I just want to go hunting and let the deer teach me how to hunt them.

Let's say you have permission to hunt 120 acres of prime deer habitat. A quick walk of the property reveals it holds classic feeding areas and secure bedding sites. You find many potential stand sites. Is it possible to have too many? Absolutely not. The more the merrier, but the key here is that you erect stands well before the season starts and be extremely picky when hunting them. The rally cry "Only when the wind is right" can never be overstated. It's not that deer always travel with their noses into the wind; that's one of deer hunting's biggest fallacies. It has more to do with travel routes. To avoid detection, the hunter must strive to place himself downwind of preferred feeding areas, travel routes and crossings. In other words, you will fool more deer if you play the percentages.

White oaks and an alder creek bottom rim one of my favorite hunting properties. The key to this spot is that it's bordered by thick pine regrowth that's part of a huge wildlife sanctuary. Can you say, "major bedding area"? I started hunting this property about eight years ago. Back then I was ultra paranoid and placed just two stands on the entire property. My success rate was good, but I soon learned I wasn't even hunting the best spots. Over the years, I've learned that deer use various parts of the hunting parcel at different times of the day and different times of the hunting season. Today, I've located hunting spots for nearly every wind direction, weather condition and time of the day. There are 12 sites in all, which include nine spots for tree stands and three natural ground blinds. As a result, I've killed deer from every nook and cranny of that property. It's almost like I can predict exactly when and where they'll

To get up close and personal with more deer, devise plans for field-side ground blinds.

appear. That confidence reduces stress and leads to more enjoyable hunting. It should be noted, however, that my ability to predict deer movement has more to do with the meticulous notes I've kept over the years than my mind-reading skills.

I use few ladder stands while bowhunting, and I never use permanent stands. These stands might be fine for gun-hunting, but I've found that older deer avoid them like the plague, especially when there's several on one property. For bowhunting, I use portable, hang-on stands and climbing sticks and/or rod-style tree steps. They're less intrusive and allow for better concealment. I also use my API climbing stand whenever possible. The climbing-stand approach offers the best first-strike approach. Select a tree several weeks in advance of a hunt, make sure there are a few natural shooting lanes nearby, and lock the stand to the base of the tree. Deer will soon accept the stand as just another piece of junk in the woods, and they'll be none the wiser when you come back to hunt ... as long as you adopt a scent-control program. Granted, not all properties are conducive to hunting with climbers, but if yours is one of them, you can drastically increase your number of stand-site options.

On the flip side, many properties only harbor one or two quality stand sites. That's OK, but it reduces a hunter's options. For example, another property I hunt consists of nothing but raspberry brush, a few mature trees and open meadows. I only have two stand sites on that property, and can only hunt it with southerly or westerly winds. Where does that leave me when October turns to November and winds are predominantly out of the north/northwest? Hunting somewhere else, that's where. I learned this lesson the hard way many years ago. If you're stubborn and continually pound a spot when wind directions aren't favorable, you'll quickly educate every deer around and gradually see fewer and fewer deer while hunting. It's a huge pain in the neck, but you have to have alternative options for stand sites if you expect to kill whitetails with any kind of consistency.

Minnesota's Pat Reeve is an outstanding buck hunter because he never relies on one method. His plans change as the season progresses.

Plan a Ground Attack

Hunting whitetails from a ground blind requires careful and calculated approaches to and from the site. Scent control is paramount. Avoid walking on deer trails leading to your ambush site, and never walk in front of the spots where you expect deer to appear. Unlike hunting from tree stands, ground-based bowhunting offers little room for error. However, the painstaking efforts are well worth the results, even if your hunt doesn't result in a filled tag. By observing deer at eye level, hunters quickly learn what will and won't work in other hunting situations.

It was a Friday afternoon in 1965 when legendary bowhunter Mel Johnson headed out to a familiar farm for a bowhunt. Although he had a few tree stands on the property, he decided on a whim to take a different approach. Deer had been pounding one of the farm's soybean fields, and he knew a brushy spot that would provide concealment and offer a good view of the afternoon's action. Best of all, the wind was blowing across the field and toward a nearby woodlot — perfect for his setup. Within a few hours, a deer stepped from the woods and headed into the field. It was about 300 yards away, but even at that distance Mel knew it was a huge buck. Long story short: The buck worked toward Mel's ambush spot, and Mel killed it cleanly with a well-placed, 20-yard shot from his 72-pound recurve.

Although that hunt took place 40 years ago, it proved a point: A bowhunter doesn't need to climb a tree to kill a whitetail. And by the way, Johnson's buck is still

HOW TO SIMPLIFY YOUR APPROACH

❦ **Pocket some peace**. Pack essentials in your jacket and pants pockets, and carry only what you'll need for each specific hunt. If you're hunting a favorite spot that's only 200 yards from the road, do you really need to bring your backpack? Probably not. Bring the essentials and leave the tools of success – field-dressing equipment, etc., back at the truck. That should give you some incentive to make a return trip later in the morning or afternoon.

❦ **Give yourself some options**. A cluttered mind can hamstring any hunter's approach. Having one or two stand sites might seem like the logical way to reduce clutter, but it actually works just the opposite. Increasing your options will reduce stress because you will no longer have to grin and bear it while worrying about wind conditions, changing deer movement patterns and potential interference from other hunters.

❦ **Be flexible**. If you only have access on small properties, select two or three ambush sites per parcel and rotate your hunting approach based solely on wind direction. Access to more than one hunting parcel will provide peace of mind by allowing for last-minute changes in hunting plans.

❦ **Get on the ground**. Not all hunting properties are conducive to tree-stand hunting. Don't overlook these parcels, because they can provide dynamite opportunities. In fact, the most successful hunters always map out one or two ground-based hunting sites for every property they hunt and only hunt it when conditions are perfect.

❦ **Don't be a one-man show**. When possible, team up with a hunting buddy. Sharing time afield not only provides for special memories, it reduces clutter by allowing friends to share notes on deer behavior and hunting tactics. This is especially helpful when hunting new properties. As they say, "Two minds are better than one."

The climbing-stand approach offers the best first-strike approach for bowhunters.

To jump on the whitetail wisdom fast track, you need to take what you already know and boil it down to the basics.

No. 1 in the Pope and Young Club's record book. Ground blinds are deadly setups for whitetails, but not all properties are conducive to hunting from the ground. Although commercial blinds might work in mature woods and some open areas, natural ambush spots are easier to select and maintain. Furthermore, natural blinds allow you to position yourself where deer travel frequently. Of course, natural blinds aren't portable and, therefore, let deer pattern you if you're not careful.

Swamps, thickets, meadows and crop fields with adjoining timber are the best places for natural blinds, and the best blinds are those that don't require a "construction project." Look for fallen trees, brush piles, tall grass or thick patches of vines, shrubs or saplings. In most of these areas, you'll find trails or crossing routes where deer invariably walk into bow range.

The best setups include a spot where you can sit with your back against a tree, stump or rock. As is the case for tree-stand hunting, a blind's most crucial ally is wind direction. When hunting crop fields, position the blind so the wind blows from the field to you. Never hunt from a field-side blind when the wind isn't right. It takes just one mistake to ruin a perfectly good spot. A deer that smells or sees a bowhunter at eye level invariably avoids that spot like the plague for the rest of the season.

After locating a potential blind, use a low-impact approach. When hunting from wind-fallen trees, a hunter need only clip a few branches and perhaps mat down some tall grass to create one or two shooting holes. Notice how I didn't say "lanes." When attempting to get within 20 yards of a whitetail at eye level, you can't afford to create large holes in the natural cover. That aspect makes ground-based bowhunting an exercise in patience. Don't expect to see the whole field or swamp. Ground-

ABOUT WIND AND THERMALS

❧ High winds are the curse of most whitetail hunters, because it seems that deer generally move less when wind speeds exceed 15 mph. This isn't true for everywhere in North America. Western whitetails, for example, live in windy conditions practically year-round. Like anything else – industrial noise, air pollution, etc. – deer are incredibly adaptive and learn to live with the environment.

It's relatively easy to select stand locations based on wind. Simply determine which direction the wind is coming from, and place stands accordingly. That approach gives you a leg up on fooling a deer's nose, but mastering wind tactics is much more complicated. That's because wind currents seldom follow the true course of the predominant direction for extended periods (hours). A good example is to imagine that you're sitting around a campfire. Although the predominant wind might be out of the west, there will be times over the course of an hour where the smoke blows in your face even though you're facing east. That's why a scent-free hunting approach is critical. Your stand might take advantage of the predominant wind for most of your hunt; it's up to you to make up the rest. Don't be fooled into thinking you can adopt a 100-percent scent-free approach. I don't think it can be done. However, if you refuse to take shortcuts, you'll be that much more likely to fool a deer's nose.

Thermals work in a similar fashion. Generally speaking, thermal air currents rise in the morning and descend in the evening. This is important knowledge for the whitetail hunter, because it helps when deciding which stands to hunt at various times of the day. Therefore, if you know where deer feed and bed throughout the day, you can put yourself in a spot to intercept them.

based bowhunting requires you enter full predator mode. Be happy with a few small shooting windows, and use your eyes and ears to do the rest.

The best natural blind I've seen is one my wife and I found while scouting along a large alfalfa field in the late 1990s. While walking the field's edge in early July, we

To tag more deer, pick out enough spots for tree stands and ground blinds so you'll have a place to hunt no matter what direction the wind blows during hunting season.

noticed a large burr oak had toppled in a recent storm. The oak's sprawling branches touched the field edge, making the tangled mess a perfect ambush location for deer that fed in the lush field. Best of all, the fallen tree was on the field's eastern edge, and the area's predominant wind blows from the southwest.

After snipping enough branches to create two basketball-sized shooting holes, we placed a black bucket aside the tree's stump. We only hunt the spot when the wind is perfect, and have killed several whitetails from it over the years, including my wife's first two bow-kills. Because she's uncomfortable in tree stands, we've used what we've learned from that blind to fashion similar blinds on our other hunting properties.

The best blinds offer good shooting opportunities in one or two directions. Don't expect your blind to offer shots in every direction. Study the site, and err on the side of camouflage, knowing that you just might have close encounters that don't result in shooting opportunities. If you do your homework and hunt smartly, a deer should be able to pass within 10 yards of your blind without knowing you're there.

The worst natural blind I've seen was one I found on public land this past fall. While scouting a dense cedar stand, I happened upon two major deer trails. The trails ran parallel to a blackberry thicket and intersected at the edge of a 3-acre opening. No mature trees were suitable for a tree stand, so I pondered hunting from a natural blind inside the thicket. Unfortunately, someone beat me to the idea. Well, sort of.

While walking to the opening, I discovered a massive ground blind just five yards from where the trails intersected. The hunter went through great pains to build this beauty. It included 8-foot limbs that had been cut with a chain saw and stacked atop each other in a crisscross fashion. The blind was about 5 feet high and had two large shooting windows facing the trails. I chuckled because I thought the guy had probably built the blind for gun season. After climbing inside, however, I realized that couldn't be the case. Maximum visibility was about 10 yards. Whoever built it must have intended to bowhunt from it!

Plan Your Approach

Hunting whitetails from a ground blind requires careful and calculated approaches to and from the site. Scent control is paramount. Avoid walking on deer trails leading to your ambush site, and never walk in front of the spots where you expect deer to appear. Adhering to these rules often requires devising an out-of-the way route.

The above-mentioned field-side blind is only 250 yards from where my wife and I park our vehicle. However, we never take a straight route to the blind, because that requires walking in front of it. Instead, we circle wide through the field, enter a pinewoods and snake our way to the blind's backside. That route requires a 20-minute walk, but it's worth the extra effort, because deer approaching the blind never cross our trail.

Making an extra effort to enter a blind is worthless without a scent-eliminating program. In the mid-1990s, I paid some attention to scent control but wasn't exactly a fanatic. That was before I met outdoor writer Gary Clancy of Minnesota. While hunting with him in western Wisconsin, he emphasized how important his total scent-control program was to his bowhunting success.

The best blinds offer good shooting opportunities in one or two directions.

Besides the standard procedures of washing hunting clothes in scent-free detergent and storing them in plastic containers, Clancy emphasizes the need for showering before every hunt and not dressing until he's out of his truck and ready to hunt. This approach is a huge inconvenience, especially when you're hunting with someone else.

I don't know how many times my wife and I received strange looks from passers-by when they saw us walking down a well-used road dressed in sweatshirts and sweat pants while carrying our bow cases and bags of hunting clothes. That's OK, because the success we've enjoyed far outweighs the "weirdoes" designation people must have assigned to us. After dressing, we douse our boots and pant legs with scent-eliminating spray. Only then are we ready to make the out-of-the-way hikes to our hunting spots.

Anyone who hunts from a tree stand knows how easy it is to "burn out" a stand by hunting it too much. The same goes for ground blinds. In fact, it's much easier to burn out a ground blind. When it comes to creating blinds, I often think back to what Myles Keller told me when I interviewed him for an article on tree-stand hunting. "If you have the property to yourself, you can never put up too many stands," he said. "Having numerous stands allows you to slip in and hunt a stand when the conditions are perfect."

It's taken a few years of legwork, but I now strictly adhere to that advice, and I don't own hunting land. What I do have is access to several small parcels of private land (less than 75 acres each) and several thousand acres of public land. In spring and summer, I pick out enough spots for tree stands and ground blinds so I'll have a place to hunt no matter what direction the wind blows during hunting season. When it's time to hunt, I only hunt from spots where the wind favors me.

Also pay attention to where the sun rises and sets in relation to your shooting lanes. A west-facing blind might be great for morning hunts, but it probably won't work for afternoon hunts. Further, try not to hunt blinds on consecutive hunts — morning and afternoon — and especially avoid hunting the same blind on consecutive days.

Try the Buddy System

Although most people view bowhunting as a solitary sport, hunters can improve their chance of success by teaming up with a partner. Whether hunting the rut or merely trying to fill some doe tags, hitting the woods with a buddy can make for an exciting hunt. However, this approach requires hunters to pay special attention to scent control, movement and noise — especially when hunting from the ground.

When hunting from the ground during the rut, it can be helpful to have one hunter call and rattle while the other hunter selects an ambush spot. Assess the situation, and keep the hunter in front of the caller at all times. You never know when or where a buck will show up. When hunting for fun, be creative. One hunter could take a video camera and climb into a tree stand while the other hunter stays on the ground near a field edge. The "spotter" can watch for approaching deer and get them on film for several minutes before the ground-based hunter gets a shooting opportunity. The result would be a video clip that forever preserves an enjoyable hunt.

I used this tactic to kill a mature doe a few years ago while hunting in Illinois with *D&DH's* Brad Rucks. Although we didn't get the whole hunt on film, the experience was priceless nonetheless. In fact, the exciting ground-based hunt has given me many ideas on how to videotape future hunts for family and friends who aren't keen on hunting from tree stands.

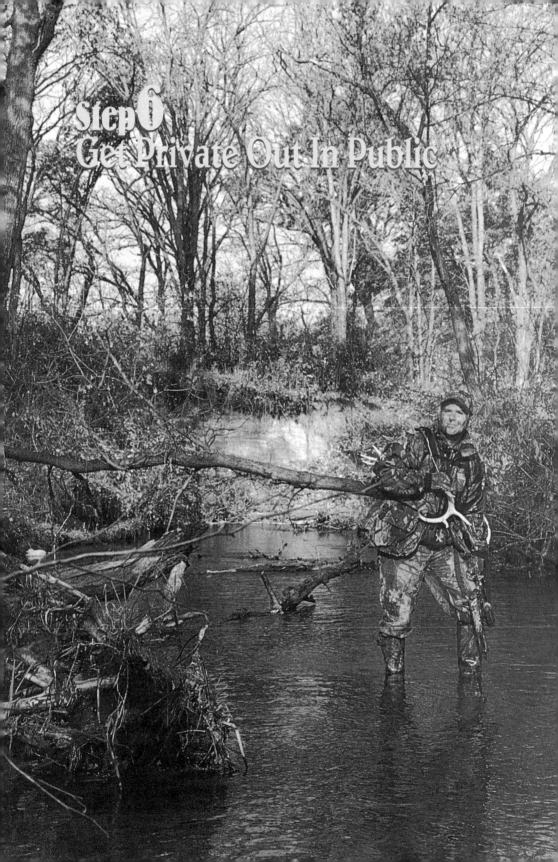

Step 6
Get Private Out In Public

My home state of Wisconsin is home to more than 15.5 million acres of forested land. However, less than 20 percent of that is open for public hunting. Consider that Wisconsin is also home to almost 700,000 gun-hunters and nearly 250,000 bowhunters, and you can easily see how competition often infiltrates the deer woods. A lot has been said and written about public hunting opportunities. In fact, some writers jump atop their pulpits and preach that public land offers fantastic opportunities for those who go the extra mile and bury themselves deep in a remote swamp, forest or river bottom.

I won't go that far. Although most of my hunting today occurs on private land, for the past 20 years I've spent many days each year hunting deer on public land. Just recently, I have noticed that going the extra mile doesn't always cut it anymore. This is especially true during gun season when, after spending an hour hiking back to your spot, you finally see daylight ... and about a dozen other orange-coats perched every 50 yards or so around your stand. Such situations aren't ideal, but they're reality. The key to dealing with them involves adapting an ever-evolving approach.

Tools of the Trade

Any serious deer hunter should obtain a general topographical overview of the land before diving headfirst into any public property. This can be done by visiting your local library and checking out the various gazetteers, plat books and topographical maps. You can really speed up the process if you're proficient with a computer mouse and keyboard.

One of the best Internet sources for free topographical maps and aerial photos is www.terraserver-usa.com. The images are provided courtesy of the United States Geographical Survey (USGS) and basically provide any deer hunter with more than enough information to thoroughly scout his hunting area. Because of security concerns, the site is sometimes refreshed and/or moved around, but it is relatively easy to navigate. The only tricky part to pinpointing specific properties is the fact you must be somewhat familiar with roads and general geographical features of the area you hunt. The aerial photos, for example, appear initially at a small scale. It is up to you to identify a road, landmark, etc., then zoom in and use your computer's mouse to navigate the countryside until you find your particular property.

Another minor Terraserver downside is that photos and topo maps are seldom up to date (most are five years old or older). Therefore, the photos will not show ecotone changes such as recently logged woodlands, etc. That's usually not a problem for most public lands, as most public properties remain untouched for decades. The beauty of aerial photos lies in the fact you can literally pore over hundreds of acres of maps in a few hours, if not minutes, from the comfort of your home or office.

Similar topo maps and aerial photos can be viewed at www.mytopo.com. The free service component of this Web site is not as detailed as the Terraserver site, but general overviews are provided. Also, Mytopo offers affordable prices on large laminated maps and glossy aerial photos of nearly all platted areas of the United

◀ **The best first-strike option for hunting public land involves locating areas with overlapping ecotones.**

No matter where you hunt, any deer taken off public land should be considered a trophy.

States. This is ideal for hunting camps. For example, you can order complete sections, then frame or tack up the maps on a camp wall and use grease pencils to indicate stand locations, etc. Maps are offered in scale ratios ranging from 1:5,000 all the way to 1:25,000. Prices vary, but an 18-by-24-inch map costs just $14.95, plus shipping.

Analyzing Ecotones

Because my tactics for scouting public land are so similar to those I use for hunting the big woods (the two are synonymous in my home state of Wisconsin), I've saved those tips for the next chapter. In a nutshell, I use an uncomplicated approach that requires paying attention to what other hunters are doing over the seasons; realizing I can't conquer a large property in just one season; and using a rather brazen push-and-probe method while scouting in the off-season.

My approach for hunting various public properties is seldom the same, because each forest is different. However, I invariably count on a few educated guesses – even gut feelings – for stand placements based on my general knowledge of an area and some pre-hunt study of an aerial map. The best first-strike options are made when hunting areas with distinct ecotones (changes in topography). My ability to find productive whitetail funnels by merely looking at a photo or map really improved when I started hunting wild turkeys. The more I learned how turkeys used certain properties, the more I realized they were leading me to deer hotspots. In fact, one of my best bucks to date came from an area I had often dismissed

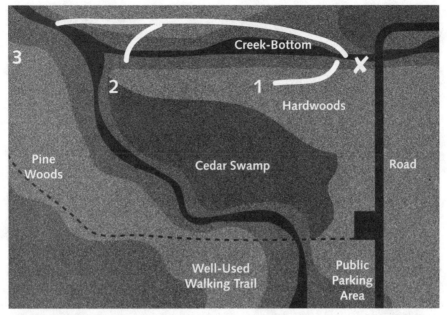

The key to public-land success often hinges on outsmarting other hunters. In this scenario, the hunter avoids the trap of using the well-used walking trail leading out of the parking area. Instead, he walks a quarter-mile north and enters on the far north property line. The three stand-site options allow the hunter to see the deer other hunters will invariably push from the southern end of the property.

because I had originally thought the surrounding woods were too nondescript to even bother hunting.

I found the spot – you guessed it – while turkey hunting. The area featured a large stand of mature white pines that gave way to some sparse red oaks and, farther north, a small tag-alder swamp. Although the pinewoods featured little understory, turkeys roosted in these monstrous trees. They'd fly up at the cusp of darkness and pitch down toward the oaks at daybreak. After observing this behavior for several days before turkey season, I realized these birds were so regular that I could have set my watch by their actions. It didn't take long to figure those birds out, and, when I did, I literally stumbled over something else – a spot for a deer stand.

Not so coincidentally, the turkeys used a deer trail to access the small oak ridge. I scouted the spot after turkey season and found a traditional rub line paralleled the trail, entering the ridge on a sideways angle through the pines. Thankfully for me, several waist-size oaks that towered 30 to 40 feet high before they branched out also bordered the trail; they were perfect for my climbing stand. Most important, however, was the fact deer entered this transition zone from the southeast and predominant autumn winds in the area are out of the west/southwest. I became even more excited when I returned home and looked at an aerial photo, which revealed a dense hemlock stand to the southeast. Bingo! With very little effort, I had pinpointed a major bedding area and a prime stand site in a subtle travel corridor.

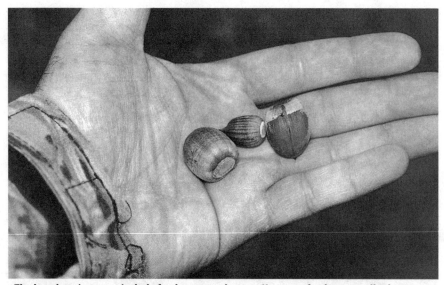

The best hunting spots include food, cover and water. However, food trumps all others when hunting low-pressured big-woods deer.

Fast-forward five months. It was the second week of archery season and I was perched in one of those arrow-straight oaks. The sun was dipping toward the tree line when I heard something snap behind me and to my left. Slowly swiveling my head, I peered over my shoulder to see a hog-fat 8-pointer standing smack-dab in the middle of the trail. He was 50 yards away and somewhat wary. He didn't smell me, but he was awfully cautious, probably because he was basically meandering through the wide-open pinewoods. He browsed, groomed himself and scanned his surroundings. This buck no doubt had just left the thick bedding cover of that hemlock stand and was just getting started on a late afternoon feeding frenzy.

I would have been content just watching that deer, but he did me the favor of eventually stepping into shooting range. My arrow found its mark, and his 135-inch rack now adorns my living-room wall. That successful hunt would have never occurred had I never been bitten by the turkey-hunting bug and insisted on analyzing how the various terrain features coincided with each other.

Converging ecotones are great spots to hunt, period. However, collectively, they are possibly the No. 1 factor to finding consistently productive spots on public land. Such areas can certainly be found through hands-on scouting, but you'll waste a lot of time and energy going that route. Use aerial photos instead, and highlight several options before hitting the woods. To make the most of your time, look for basic overlapping areas, such as:

1. Conifer swamps and mature hardwoods. These are the easiest places to pinpoint deer activity, because dense swamps provide cover for pressured deer. No matter where you are, pressured deer will use cover to bed and move throughout the day.

Some public hunting areas also include sanctuaries. Be sure you know the boundaries before the season.

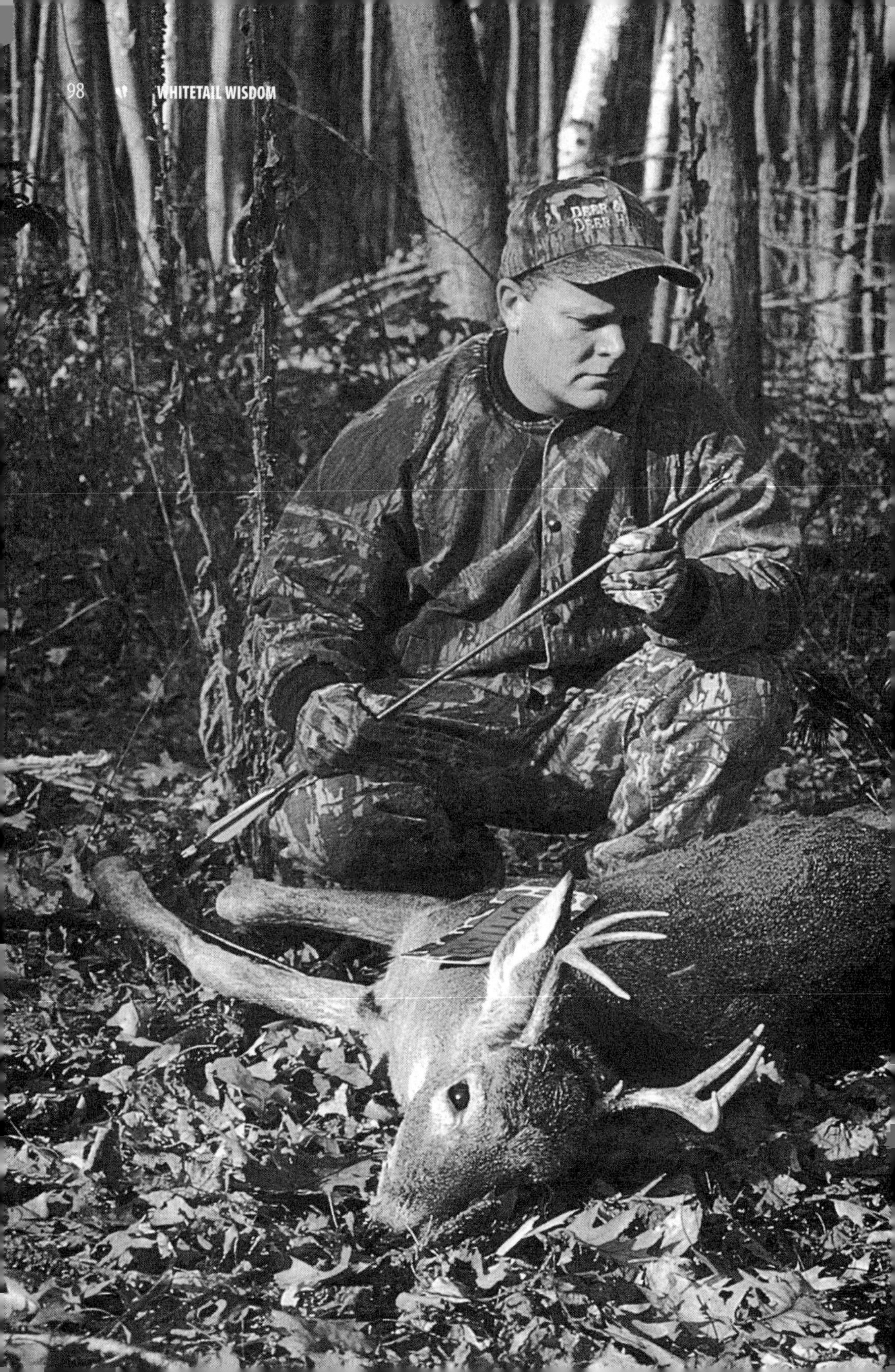

HOW TO GET PRIVATE OUT IN PUBLIC

❦ **Give yourself some options.** You won't find consistent success by pounding the same spot on the same property hunt after hunt, year after year. Public land is abundant. Therefore, you should have a plan that provides up to five backup spots in case someone beats you to your favorite stand site.

❦ **Point and click.** Make the most out of modern technology by relying on the Internet and the various free-access mapping programs.

❦ **Actively seek converging ecotones.** Such areas can certainly be found through hands-on scouting, but you'll waste a lot of time and energy going that route. Use maps and aerial photos to get pointed in the right direction.

❦ **Never dismiss a thick tangle, swamp or marshy area.** Deer grow to maturity by seeking such areas and holding tight in them until hunting pressure decreases.

❦ **Have a short memory.** Just because someone finds your favorite spot doesn't mean you've lost it forever. The majority of public-land hunters are casual whitetail enthusiasts who show up for a few days each fall. Consistent success comes to those who learn ways to hunt around the crowds and don't let a few setbacks curb their enthusiasm.

Dragging your deer out of the woods for all to see is a sure way to lose an otherwise "secret" spot.

2. Creek bottoms and hardwoods. Bottoms provide everything a deer needs to survive: food, water and cover. Hardwood ridges also provide food, and, depending on pressure, ideal bedding areas. Unpressured deer often prefer ridges as bedding areas, because the elevated terrain allows them to better position themselves to scan their surroundings and take advantage of thermals. In fact, deer generally bed on the highest ground they can find and feed at lower elevations.

3. Mature woods and logged areas. Deer love edges, especially where thick new growth borders old growth. These become natural travel corridors, especially in nondescript areas consisting of thousands of acres of otherwise unbroken forest.

4. High points and low points. Some areas, especially national forests with low deer densities, consist of nothing more than mile after mile of mature forest. These areas are extremely difficult to hunt, but success can be had when a hunter keys off of subtle ecotone changes, such as high ridges; saddles between ridges; strips of cover between wilderness lakes; and ditches, drainages and dry riverbeds.

When hunting any piece of public land, never dismiss a thick tangle, swamp or marshy area. If you think an area seems "too wet" to hold deer, think again. Deer grow to maturity by seeking such areas and holding tight in them until hunting pressure decreases.

Deer love edges, especially where new growth borders mature forests.

This is the author's remedy for taking a deer out of the woods without leaving a blood trail for others to follow.

Never Curb Your Enthusiasm

Learning terrain features and how deer use them is the easy part, or at least should be the fun part, of hunting public properties. Keeping a positive attitude in the face of adversity is the hard part.

Outdoor writer Steve Bartylla is a master at outsmarting big bucks on public land. During a recent conversation on private-land hunting, he told me, "Unless you own the land, you're bound to lose your best hunting spots at some point in your life. That's why you always need an ace in the hole." No truer words have ever been uttered, and I believe the same advice holds true for public land. No matter how remote – how "secret" – you think your spot is, someone else is bound to find it and horn in on it.

Losing public-land honey holes to other hunters happened to my family, friends and me many times over when we hunted Wisconsin's North Woods during the state's annual firearms season. I found one spot by accident while grouse hunting one fall, and we proceeded to kill two dandy bucks and a doe from this hideaway that season. It was a great spot, but we were naïve in that we didn't safeguard it closely enough. We parked our trucks at the trail's head leading to the spot, and we dragged our deer straight out to the road during daylight. It didn't take long for other hunters to flock to the area like ravens to a steaming gut pile. At the time, we were ticked off at the brazenness of some of these hunters. One guy literally walked in on my brother-in-law and banged his climbing stand up a tree just 50 yards from "our" spot. Of course, he had as much right to hunt the land as we did, so we pulled out and hunted other spots.

Such intrusions rarely last. Sure, we lost that spot for a few seasons, but the other hunters eventually made enough careless mistakes (scent control issues, etc.) to render the spot unproductive. Unfortunately, we have all since moved on, and no one hunts that spot anymore. It's not that it's burned out. In fact, it's probably just as good as it was when I found it. The area consists of a lush riverbottom bordered by aspen regrowth and a dense spruce and black fir thicket. And now that the pressure is off, I'll bet my Buck knife that deer have resumed "normal operations." This is common deer behavior on public land. Pressure them too much, and they'll temporarily vacate an area. The key word there is "temporary." It is almost physically impossible to permanently alter deer behavior, unless, of course, you build a shopping mall in their bedding, feeding or travel areas!

The moral? Have backup plans. This should go beyond designating a stand site that is, say, 300 yards from your favorite spot. Think outside the box. Most public lands are vast. Scout areas that require some driving time, and select second, third, fourth and even fifth next-best spots that are just as good as Option 1. It might be a pain in the neck and require you hunt off times – midday, etc. – but such planning invariably results in a much more enjoyable ... and productive ... hunt.

Keep Your Secrets!

We all take pride in our deer hunting accomplishments. It adds to the sporting experience and enhances camp camaraderie. After all, you've worked hard for months to figure out how deer are using a certain property, and then had the wherewithal to drop the hammer or release the arrow at precisely the right time. Do this on public land, and you're ready to shout it from the mountains for all to hear.

Not so fast! Consistent success on public-land whitetails requires a hunter to adopt a cool-as-a-cucumber attitude. By all means, tell others of your accomplishment and don't be shy to show your deer to whoever wants to see it. However, don't be stupid and tell others exactly where you shot it ... unless, of course, you want company next time around! If all is indeed fair in love and war, it also has to apply to hunting public land.

In the beginning of this book, I made special mention of my family and friends who belong to the Coffee Lake Hunting Club. In reality, the camp's name was a self-imposed moniker we coined in the 1980s when we were feebly trying to waylay whitetails on public land. The gun season was half over, and our six-man group had put just one deer – a 70-pound doe fawn – up on the meat pole. Deer sightings were few, and we were depressed beyond belief. It was lunchtime when we headed to the cabin of a longtime family friend. You can only imagine the expressions on our faces when we pulled into the driveway and saw three mature bucks hanging from their meat pole.

Back then, we all possessed a little – OK, a lot – of apple-cheeked innocence. "Where did you guys get all of those bucks?" I gasped as one of the hunters stepped out on the porch. "Two of them came from right here around the cabin, and the big one was shot just north of the lake." Talk about an energy boost. We wolfed down our sandwiches and sodas and immediately sped back to camp to analyze our plat books.

After a few minutes of deliberations, we decided to drive – yes, make a deer drive in a huge chunk of national forest – what we thought was a thin strip of cover alongside Coffee Lake. Long story short, there was fresh snow that day when my buddy and I (the drivers) set off through toward the standers. We walked for three hours across what was basically the moon's surface, sans the craters. We made that drive two more times the next season with the same result: no deer tracks or sign whatsoever. The fruitless jaunts, despite giving us sore feet and nighttime charley horses, did provide some value. We finally had a name for our camp and a specific location to tell people where we shot all of our deer!

Stick With the Plan

You have several things going for you as a serious whitetail hunter: You want to succeed so badly that you'll do whatever it takes to accomplish the goal. This attitude is absolutely necessary when hunting public land, or even private land that abuts public ground. That means devising a game plan and sticking with it no matter what happens on the way to your stand, or whatever weather Mother Nature cooks up.

Nothing will get deer up and moving better than a changing barometer, especially when a looming front is bringing cool showers with it. Such was the case when I was hunting a small, private lease I had a few years ago. The lease was bordered by more than 1,000 acres of remote public land that's home to lots of big bucks.

Despite otherwise pleasant conditions, the late-morning forecast called for steadily dropping temperatures and thunderstorms. I absolutely hate bowhunting in the rain and, in fact, seldom go when I know rain is imminent. It not only makes for miserable hunting, but it can wash away a blood trail in a hurry. However, something told me I could hunt a few hours before worrying about it.

I couldn't help but think about the forthcoming rainstorm as I walked the logging road toward my stand. I was probably too preoccupied with those thoughts as I crested a rise and unhooked a log chain from a metal gate. As I closed it, the dew-soaked gate slipped through my fingers and slammed into some brush. "Clank!" Within seconds, three deer crashed past my stand site and bounded deep into the public forest. "Nice. Real nice," I scolded myself. "Might as well turn around and go home now." Something prevented me from leaving. Still, I slumped my shoulders and skulked the remaining 100 yards to my stand site.

Most of the trees in that forest were at least 50 years old and straight as arrows. They were grown for saw logs, but they made for mighty fine hunting trees for a guy with a climber. After tiptoeing up the ridge, I stepped onto my stand, fastened my safety line and started climbing. The stand's rubber-coated bicycle chain gripped

An ATV is the ultimate tool for getting a deer out of the woods quickly and efficiently.

the bark solidly without making any noise. At least I would get into hunting position without making much more noise, or so I thought. "Clunk!"

"What the?" I hissed as the top part of the climber hit something solid. I peered around the tree and noticed a long, calf-sized limb. I didn't have a handsaw, and daylight was nearing. I was stuck – just 12 feet off the ground. I had to set up shop right there whether I liked it or not. Making matters worse, sweat was now pouring off my forehead. The fact I was downwind of the deer trail was the only thing that kept me from leaving. "Got to stay put," I told myself while settling in. "You just never know."

The day's first rays of sunlight glinted through the treetops when several deer appeared on a distant logging road and scooted into the woods I was hunting. I spied the movement of a big doe and two fawns when they were about 100 yards in front of my stand. They were heading my way, munching on acorns and nipping browse. It took a few minutes for them to close within 40 yards. I firmly believe that any deer taken while bowhunting is a trophy, so I stood slowly, swiveled my hips and watched the big doe's every move. Unfortunately, she stalled and eventually veered off the trail and out of bow range. That's when I saw more movement and ... antlers!

Like a dream, a giant buck appeared on the ridge and trotted steadily down the trail. Within seconds, he stepped within 18 yards of my stand. The buck dipped his head and plucked an acorn from the ground. He worked it like a piece of chewing gum while scanning the woods. My heart hammered as I came to full draw and let

PUBLIC-LAND BUCKS: MISSION POSSIBLE!

I consider myself blessed to have a job that allows me to routinely tap the minds of North America's top deer hunters. Every one of them is an expert hunter in his own right, but some stand out above the crowd because of their common-man upbringings and subsequent successes while hunting public land.

At the risk of making a good friend feel old, I will note that Michigan's Richard Smith was killing big whitetails on public land before I was even born. He has hunted whitetails in nearly every state and province and says, despite increased hunting pressure, hunters can routinely succeed if they put their minds to it. "I've killed six deer on public land in Michigan over the past 10 years," Smith said. "So, it can still be done." His best public-land buck ever came from land owned by the U.S. Forest Service. It was a 5 1/2-year-old 10-pointer that netted 148 Boone-and-Crockett inches.

Other familiar names include Wisconsin's Doug Below, who arrowed a 155-inch buck from public land near his home in 2002, and New York's Bill Vaznis, who recently killed a 140-class 9-pointer on state-owned land in Iowa. However, Virginia's Walt Hampton is possibly the be-all expert. Since 1994, he has taken 88 deer off of public land throughout the Southeast. His secret? "Locate military bases that allow open hunting. They have tons of deer!" Although Hampton is not in the habit of measuring the bucks he kills, he estimates his best public-land buck is a 156-inch 11-pointer he shot a few years ago.

Michigan's John Eberhart is another proficient public-land hunter, having killed six trophy bucks off heavily hunted state land in the past 10 years. "I personally believe there is a huge difference from state land to state land, depending on what state you hunt in," said Eberhart. "State land in highly populated states is much, much more difficult to hunt than state lands in non-pressured states. For example, my son Chris hunted state land in Michigan for 18 years and has seen one Pope-and-Young-caliber buck. Just recently, he hunted state land in Montana. In just two days, he saw four P&Y bucks, and that was in September!"

All it takes is one success story for most public-land hunters to keep the faith.

the arrow fly. The buck mule-kicked, whirled and sprinted in the direction from which he had come. He didn't go far, and I was soon tying my tag on the antlers of my first Pope-and-Young-class whitetail.

Yes, luck definitely plays a part in many successful hunts. However, sticking with the game plan – no matter how many things go wrong on a given morning or afternoon – is often the key to success.

step 7
Break Down The Big Woods

Why does every big-woods deer camp seem to have one or two guys who go years without killing – much less seeing – big deer? Simple. They don't hunt hard enough, and they often have a negative attitude. Hunters too often fall into routines by hunting the same unproductive areas. That approach, coupled with the tendency to blame other hunters and state deer managers for a perceived lack of deer, doesn't help fill tags. By taking control of your own destiny and formulating a well-thought-out plan, you can find more and bigger deer in huge public forests … no matter if you hunt in Virginia, Wisconsin, Ontario, Maine or anywhere in between. This chapter will break down the mystery of the big woods and explain simple tactics you can use immediately to improve your odds for success.

Tackling a New Environment

We had to be crazy. It was the third day of gun season, and we were lining up for a deer drive in one of the most mature pine forests in northern Wisconsin. My dad dropped my best friend and me off at a logging road, and then headed up the road with my brother to take him to his stand. My brother gave me a thumbs-up and a hopeful smile as they drove away.

"I don't know why we're even bothering," I said to my buddy. "There ain't any deer here anyway."

Despite my pessimism, I told my buddy to walk 300 yards down the trail and wait for my signal – an owl hoot – before beginning his slow walk toward the standers. I let 10 minutes pass and then hooted. My buddy and I had walked maybe 100 yards when the crack of a .30-06 shattered the morning's silence. The shot came from my dad's direction. My heart hammered and I quickened my pace.

Boom! Another shot echoed through the woods. By then, I must have looked like a pumpkin jogging through the woods. Within minutes, I crested a spruce-covered hill to see my dad and brother hugging each other and exchanging high-fives. Beside them, in 4 inches of fresh snow, was a mammoth white-tailed buck. To my surprise, the buck was one of several deer bedded in the mature section of that woods. In the decades since, we've discovered loads of deer in similar big-woods habitats. So much for the "ain't-any" theory.

Before my journalism days, I was somewhat skeptical of deer population estimates by my state's game agency. No more. After working with deer managers from every state in the country for the past 10 years, I have learned that most states, especially my home state of Wisconsin, are highly adept at estimating deer populations, especially in the big woods of the North. Wisconsin, however, is a prime example of how accurately managers can estimate deer herds, because the Badger State is one of the few that still requires hunters to register every deer they kill. Most other states rely on estimates, which are usually educated guesses. Wisconsin has a long history of annually estimating its overall harvest within 5 percent, and sometimes even better than that. With such accurate accounting, managers can use proven scientific formulas to calculate herd numbers.

◀ **If you're the type of hunter who has become accustomed to seeing deer on every hunt, big-woods hunting might not be for you.**

Pinpointing subtle changes in topography is the key to unraveling deer travel patterns across large, unbroken tracts of forest.

The problem with states like Wisconsin, however, lies in the fact that it consists of highly varied habitat. The North Woods is only suitable for low deer densities, whereas the southern farmlands can accommodate densities in excess of 40 deer per square mile. These differences require hunters to adopt drastically different hunting tactics.

Most big-woods environments harbor deer densities of less than 20 deer per square mile, and some have fewer than 5 deer per square mile. Conversely, some farmlands and central woodland areas have three to five times that many deer. So, tactics that work in northern Iowa and southern Illinois probably won't work in places like Canada, Maine and northern Wisconsin. I have hunted each of those regions and learned the hard way. However, I've also discovered three tactics that consistently lead me to big-woods deer.

Don't Try to Conquer All

Large tracts of big woods typically include fantastic deer habitat, but they also consist of thousands, if not millions, of acres of unproductive deer land. Although I hunted and dearly loved the Chequamegon National Forest for nearly 20 years, I learned that many parts of it are a Dead Sea for deer. The same can be said of the big national forests and lumber-company lands in the Southeast and Northeast.

Don't waste time hunting large tracts of mature woods. That approach can be productive, but it's more frustrating and futile. Instead, hunt areas where young and old growth meet, and scout from your truck whenever possible. Use a county plat book, and begin by marking an "X" at your camp. From there, break down the map into sections – 640 acres – and continue by investigating each section in a 10-mile radius. This might take weeks, but it's worthwhile.

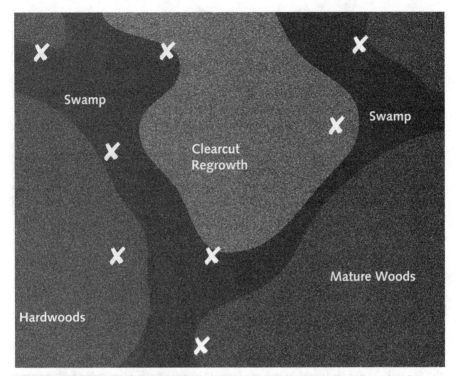

Not all big-woods environments have much topographical structure, but those that do provide fantastic hunting opportunities. This scenario shows an overview of the author's favorite big-woods spot, which happens to sprawl in a heavily hunted national forest. The best stand sites (shown with Xs) are the pinch points where ecotones overlap.

Drive each road and logging trail, looking for deer habitat. Deer trails that cross roads are good starting places, but it's even wiser to note areas that include young aspen clearcuts, pine plantations, cedar swamps or any amount of red or black oaks. In wilderness areas, note streams, rivers, ponds and hiking/snowmobile trails.

I have often combined road-scouting efforts with annual spring and summer fishing trips, when lush foliage helps contrast well-worn deer trails that zigzag from fresh understory to river bottoms and swamp edges. In desperate times, hunters can find deer by paying attention to who's baiting (where legal). Unfortunately, many people have abused baiting regulations recently, and by the time gun season arrives, bare-path deer trails lead from dense swamps to open high ground.

Nonbaiters can find deer by hunting bedding areas where corn-fed deer seek refuge. That might not sound like much fun, but, unfortunately, it's usually a hunter's only option when his neighbors insist on breaking the rules. Despite baiting, bowhunters can always find good action at natural food sources. Like most whitetails, big-woods deer don't miss the opportunity to dine on acorns and clearcut browse when it's abundant. Look for young stands of maple, big-tooth aspen, black spruce, and white and gray poplar.

Most big-woods environments harbor deer densities of less than 20 deer per square mile, and some have fewer than 5 deer per square mile.

In areas where young growth isn't abundant, look for natural runways near creeks, depressions, beaver dams and rock formations. Some of the best deer hunting in the big woods can be found in remote funnels between lakes, swamps and rivers. A topographical map is critical to pinpointing these areas. Unfortunately, finding one or two such areas isn't enough. Success hinges on flexibility, especially if you hunt public land.

It's wise to find at least three walking routes, three ground-blind sites and five to seven good spots for tree stands. Many options let you plan hunts based on weather, food source availability and the presence of other hunters. In the big woods, it's easy to devise endless options. However, the task is more difficult in the central woodlands and southern farmlands. Hunters in those areas can expand their options by investigating public land, forest crop land and land enrolled in a managed forest program. Contact your state's fish and game department for more information on forest crop and managed forest programs.

Be Snoopy

Without a doubt, the big woods can be big-time intimidating. Most first-time hunters make mistakes by tackling massive forests with the conquer-all attitude. That approach usually spells trouble, and it can make the task a five-year project. That's why there's nothing wrong with playing the part of a private investigator. In other words, let someone else show you where to hunt.

I've used the "snooping" tactic several times over the years to find new hunting spots. Don't get me wrong: I don't home in on another hunter's turf. I merely pay close attention to where they hunt. For example, in the late 1990s, my buddy and

The sight of a big buck is usually enough to keep a big-woods hunter focused on the task at hand.

I were on our way to our favorite bowhunting spot when we passed a familiar logging road that led to an old clearcut. The road was overgrown with weeds, and small aspen shoots nearly covered the entrance.

"Remember those two guys that always parked there on opening day?" my buddy said. "I haven't seen them in a while. I wonder what's back there."

We didn't wonder for long. I stopped the truck, turned around and headed for the logging road. "Let's find out," I said.

We left our gear in the truck and grabbed a compass. After scouting the area for two hours, we realized we had found another hotspot. The old clearcut was thick and difficult to enter, but its edge was littered with deer sign. During the gun season, my buddy was set up off the logging road when he had a close encounter with a 130-class buck. I didn't have to ask him where he'd be bowhunting the next season.

Opening day of gun season is one of the best times to observe what's going on over a large area of big woods. Ask yourself a few questions, and you'll learn a lot about the area and how deer use it. Where is everyone hunting? Where did those shots come from? Where did someone drag out a deer? Answer those questions, and you will find more deer. Most hunters don't have the time or patience to spend the whole gun season in the forest. Make mental notes on where they hunt opening weekend, and revisit those spots daily. You should have them to yourself midway through opening week.

Powerline right-of-ways provide abundant regrowth, which deer use for food and cover throughout the season.

Besides driving and observing where other hunters enter the woods, I pay attention to conversations when I'm at restaurants, grocery stores and gas stations. A simple statement like, "Joe Smith got a real nice buck over by Coffee Lake," might be general or even a lie, but you can bet I'll drive past the area to check it out. In fact, this snooping tactic has paid off more than once for my hunting partners and me. That's the beauty of hunting remote forests. They are large enough and most of the land is public. What's more, the chances of bumping into another hunter while hunting are slim, and you can always move a few ridges over if someone gets to a good spot before you.

Push and Probe

Don't be intimated by pre-season scouting. Although it doesn't hurt, you don't have to spend lots of time in the woods to learn where and when deer are active. One of the best ways to scout land quickly is what I call the push-and-probe technique. It's best to tackle new territory right after the gun season, but that approach isn't necessary if you merely want to find deer.

The push-and-probe tactic isn't difficult. Pick a chunk of land and walk it – fast. Look for trails and other deer sign, and intentionally try to spook deer. Again, this is best done after the season. Spooking deer during the season might trigger them to change their habits. Deer sign should tell you where deer go when disturbed. I've found some great hotspots when using this tactic in early December, because snow tells all.

This aggressive approach isn't wise for big-buck haunts. However, spring and summer push-and-probe operations usually help find early bow-season stand sites without adversely affecting deer patterns. Another word of caution: Don't overdo it. The idea is to get a quick read on the areas deer frequent. Use the hunting season to figure out the rest of the equation.

Hunting Logged Areas

Hunting the big woods requires much determination and persistence, especially if you're used to hunting areas with high deer densities. If you're the type of hunter who has become accustomed to seeing deer on every outing, big-woods hunting might not be for you. It can be an extremely rewarding experience, but it takes an attitude adjustment. Seeing more deer isn't always better in the big woods, and, in fact, less is probably better, because the few deer you will see are usually of high quality. Still, if the big woods are your only option for hunting, and you need to see deer, focus on clearcuts. They will be your best option for seeing more deer more often.

Although the word clearcut is almost a dirty word in today's tree-hugging climate, it shouldn't be. Clearcuts and select cuts are invariably the result of sound timber and wildlife management. Mature, park-like woodlands are pretty to walk through, but they offer little in the way of habitat for wildlife. Despite the stigmatism, clearcuts can still be found, especially in areas of the North, Northeast and Southeast where timber companies control literally millions of acres of land.

HOW TO BREAK DOWN THE BIG WOODS

Learn how to dissect. Don't waste time hunting large tracts of mature woods. Instead, hunt areas where young and old growth meet, and do most of the scouting from your truck. Mark potential spots on a plat book, then further analyze the topography back at camp with maps and/or aerial photos.

In wilderness areas, note streams, rivers, ponds and snowmobile trails. Consider visiting your deer hunting area for a fishing trip in spring or summer. Use the down time to do some scouting. Something as simple as driving back roads and making mental notes of well-worn deer trails can go a long way toward a filled deer tag come fall.

Spy on other hunters. Study what they do and when they do it. It's not about stealing their spots; it's about learning where the deer are. From there, you can eliminate unproductive areas. This tactic can shave years off the big-woods learning curve.

Push and probe. Don't be intimated by pre-season scouting. Although it doesn't hurt to spend a lot of time in the woods, pick and choose your spots and scout them on weekends. Tackle new territory right after the gun season when deer sign is fresh – giving you a better indication of how deer use the land during the time that matters most.

Don't waste time. Pick a chunk of land and walk it – fast. Look for deer trails and other sign, and intentionally try to spook deer. Deer sign will tell you where deer have been, but the real thing will tell you where they go when disturbed.

Bowhunters are best served when they hunt young clearcuts, especially those that are 1 to 4 years old.

Hunting clearcuts requires some scouting legwork. The best pieces for deer hunting are young cuts – anywhere from 1 to 7 years old. Young clearcuts provide abundant browse, travel cover and bedding areas for whitetails. When scouting, look for well-worn trails and terrain features such as hillsides, creek bottoms and areas where tree species overlap. One of the best clearcuts I've ever hunted included a vast poplar ridge that tapered down toward a mature conifer stand. The edge habitat along that ridge provided fantastic travel corridors for deer, which browsed in the poplar slash during the day and bedded in the dense canopy of the conifers in the evening. Such edges can also become hotspots for buck activity during the rut. On that particular edge, for example, I found countless rubs and scrapes over the years.

Bowhunters are best served when they hunt young cuts, especially those that are 1 to 4 years old. Early season action can be incredible because deer are easier to pattern, as they have likely browsed the same areas in summer. Gun-hunters, on the other hand, should seek older clearcuts (3 to 6 years), because the resulting slash provides deer more cover and security when October turns to November and all the trees become devoid of leaves. Nearly all clearcuts feature thick regrowth coupled with scattered "sentinel" trees. Loggers spare these mature trees for various reasons, but you can rest assured that deer key off of them big time. Investigate as many sentinels as you can while scouting, and you'll likely discover deer trails running past them. These trees make for great stand sites, especially when using a climbing tree stand during gun season.

CLEARCUT WAYS TO BETTER DEER HUNTING

The size, shape and distribution of clearcuts have major effects on many species of wildlife, not just white-tailed deer. True, timber companies, state agencies and the federal government use clearcuts to generate income, but the greater good is that such efforts create brand-new forests. Due to public pressure, however, large clearcuts are becoming much less common. Most of today's clearcuts are measured in 40-acre blocks, not square miles.

Clearcuts are especially beneficial to deer populations, and hunting greatly improves in the years following a major cut. The best spots for hunting are areas where foresters leave strips of uncut timber between adjacent clearcuts. These timbered corridors might only be 100 yards wide, but they provide excellent transition areas for deer. Likewise, small islands of standing timber within clearcuts provide staging and bedding areas for deer as they move from the clearcut to nearby mature forests.

According to a report by Virginia State University, clearcutting may be the only practical way to enhance wildlife habitat in areas of poor soil fertility and dry conditions. Under these conditions, the report said clearcutting timber for firewood or pulp for paper mills is frequently the only economically feasible timber management system available to increase the amount of early succession forest for wildlife habitat.

Hunting Water Sources

Hunting near big-woods ponds, lakes, streams and rivers can be productive, but it requires a somewhat different approach then when hunting farmland water sources. Big-woods deer usually don't have to travel far to find water, so these areas aren't usually magnets for deer activity. I've killed few deer when hunting right on top of a big-woods water source. In fact, it took many years for me to kick the habit of finding a well-worn water-source trail and popping up a tree stand within shooting range of where deer drank.

A better tactic for hunting big-woods water sources is to set up in natural corridors leading to and from the area. My hunting partners and I have bagged many whitetails by hunting natural runways between small wilderness lakes and rivers. In fact, one of my most memorable hunts came in the late 1980s when I killed a buck that used a thick strip of tamarack swamp to navigate his way between a 10-acre pond and a 50-acre lake. The corridor between the water sources was only 100 yards wide, but it was extremely thick. I found my stand site, which was a flat rock atop a nearby ridge, by scouting the area in late September. Find secluded waterways, and you'll typically find terrain that's littered with prime edge habitat. Deer gravitate toward water, making edge corridors top spots for ambush locations.

After locating a prime location, analyze the area and document all of its features in a notebook, or highlight them on a topographical map. Post-season scouting is best, but the same work can be done during a "flyer" hunt during the season. Carefully dissect the area and determine how the predominant winds move through the huntable spots. Next, locate potential stand sites; making sure you can hunt them without being winded by cruising deer. A key to hunting big-woods water sources is to disregard them as destinations for deer to come and drink. Deer use these areas more for the succulent browse and excellent bedding cover they provide.

The twigs and leaves of big-tooth aspen is a preferred deer browse in the North Woods.

Step 1 Become a student of whitetail wisdom by studying deer behavior.

Step 2 Speed up the learning process by scouting less and hunting more.

Step 3 Think like a deer by knowing why they use certain areas at various times of the season.

Step 4 Play above the competition by learning how, when and where to hunt pressured deer.

Step 5 Simplify your approach by devising a well-thought-out game plan for every property you hunt.

Step 6 Find more deer on public land by going the extra mile to find areas other hunters overlook.

Step 7 Break down the big woods by syudying subtle terrain features.

Step 8 Hone your hunting skills by taking advantage of liberal doe-hunting seasons.

Step 9 Become a buck hunter by measuring up to your — not someone else's — standards of what is a trophy.

Step 10 Shoot like a pro through regular practice before, after and during hunting season.

Step 11 Become a utilitarian by leaving the gadgets at home.

When hunting the big woods, pay attention to all deer sign — no matter where you find it.

up on opening day. Ask any of today's top big-woods hunters – Richard Smith, Doug Below, Claudio Ongaro, John Eberhart and Greg Miller, to name a few – and they'll tell you endless stories about how they have routinely sat – dark to dark – for days on end without seeing a single deer. These guys prevail, however, because they adopt that never-say-never attitude and stick it out till the bitter end. And, invariably, they wind up driving home with big bucks in the back of their pickup trucks.

The proper big-woods mindset requires that a hunter set his watch to "deer time." Stop worrying about the work you left behind at the office, how badly the yard needs to be raked and mowed and how you're going to get all those bills paid and to the post office by next Monday. This is your time to hunt. Forget about everything else, focus on the task at hand and, above all, relax a little. Five 12-hour days in the deer woods will be physically taxing, but it certainly beats five 12-hour days behind a steering wheel, factory machine or corporate computer screen.

Keep that mental edge by packing plenty of water and high-energy snacks like raisins, nuts, granola bars and fruit. You'll stay more alert and be less tired at the end of the day. Avoid high-fat foods and junk food like chocolate, chips and sugared soft drinks. Especially avoid excessive amounts of caffeine. Coffee or Pepsi might wake you up temporarily, but the effect won't last and will actually make you more tired later in the day. It may be bland and boring, but nothing beats plain old water.

Step 8
Match Wits With A Matriarch

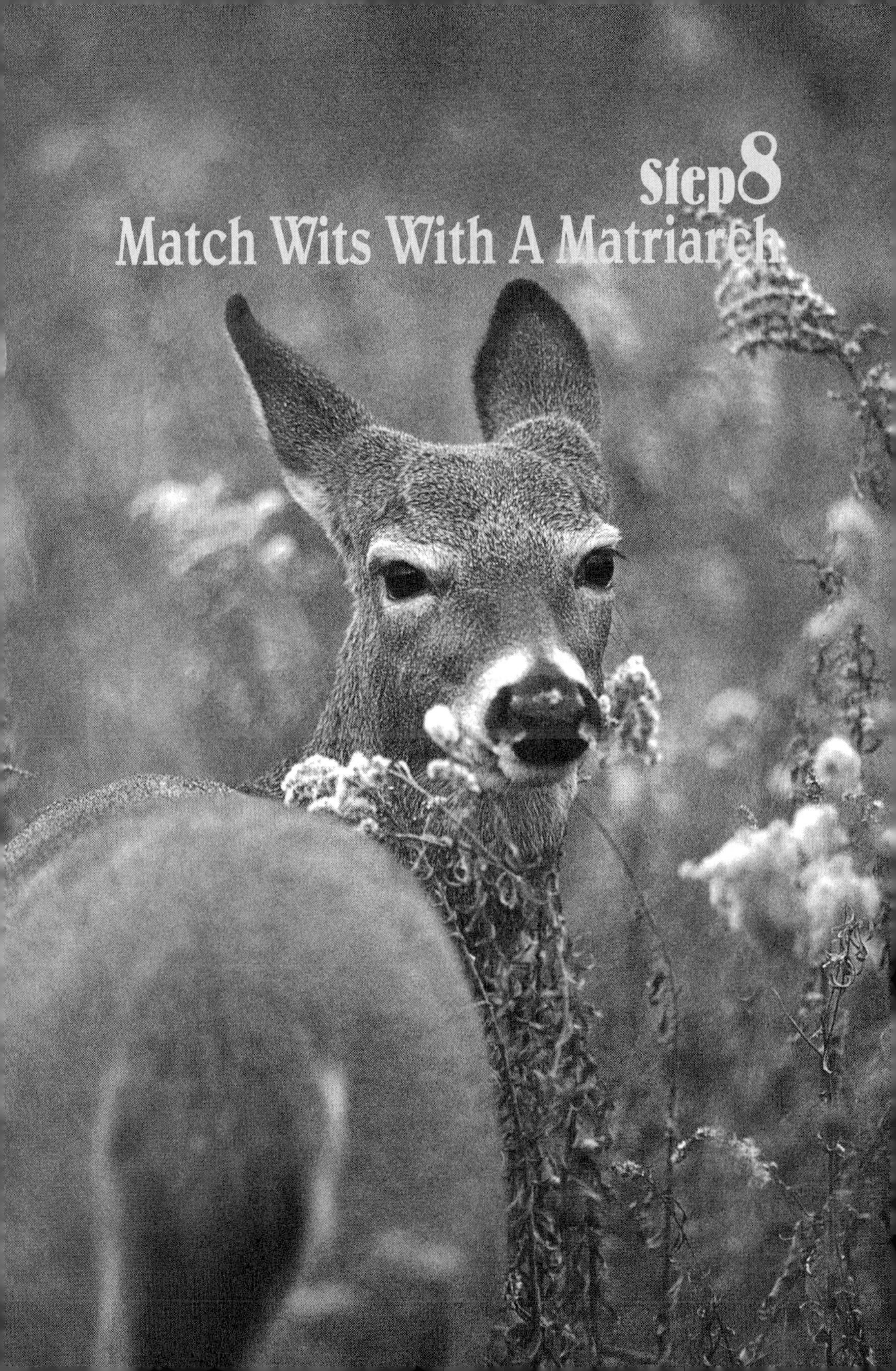

I am blessed to know some incredible deer hunters. And, despite becoming famous for their big-buck exploits, guys like Charles Alsheimer, Bob Zaiglin, Walt Hampton, Dick Bernier, Richard Smith, Doug Below and Ted Nugent still fight the good fight of preaching the importance of being a good land steward first and foremost. They know that hunting antlerless deer not only provides invaluable experience for staying atop hunting's never-ending learning curve, it sends an important message to nonhunters – the key electorate to hunting's future – that hunters provide an invaluable public service.

Indeed, today's deer hunters are victims of media overplay. Videos, television shows and magazine articles glorify mature white-tailed bucks as kings of the woods. That's debatable. Although big bucks are certainly crafty, they don't have anything on wise, old does. In fact, I'll stick my neck out and say mature does are the smartest deer in the woods. Think about that for a minute. A mature buck only has to look out for himself, and, even then, he becomes unglued at least once every hunting season — during the rut. The same cannot be said for a fully mature doe. She's always on high alert, probably because she usually has to watch out for more than just herself. With fawns usually in tow, a matriarch is often the leader of the pack when doe groups congregate. Add it up, and it makes for an ultra-wary critter.

Hunting The Horse

The best example of a hard-to-kill doe that I've ever seen was a whitetail my wife and I encountered while bowhunting in the late 1990s. Tracy had a close encounter with the doe during the third week of archery season. The doe was so big that we nicknamed it The Horse.

It was a cool September afternoon, and Tracy was nestled in her favorite ground blind, overlooking an alfalfa field and a creek crossing. As the afternoon passed, a

Second-time mothers are considered "dispersers," because they usually leave their birthing areas and move a quarter-mile or more to find a new home territory.

Taking a mature doe should be considered quite an accomplishment, especially when done at close range with a bow and arrow.

combination of eight does and fawns appeared and fed across the field. The Horse was the final deer in the procession. Although the other deer walked within bow range of Tracy's blind, the big doe never stepped closer than 40 yards. In fact, when she first entered the field, the doe came on a dead run, stopping abruptly when she was about 75 yards into the field — classic behavior of an older deer that's survived a few hunting seasons.

Tracy didn't shoot a deer that afternoon because she had her sights set on that big doe. We saw The Horse several more times that fall, but neither of us unleashed an arrow. I assumed I could kill that doe during firearms season, but I never saw it. It reappeared in mid-December, and I could soon distinguish it from other deer. Its size alone was a telltale factor, but its double throat patch made it readily identifiable.

We observed The Horse for two more hunting seasons without ever getting a shot at it. What made this deer almost impossible to kill? Several things actually:

1. The doe bedded in a state park, which is a wildlife sanctuary.

2. The doe always entered our hunting property from a downwind position.

3. The doe almost always entered the field as shooting time expired.

4. The doe was very high-strung and oftentimes would go on high alert and flee back into the sanctuary for no apparent reason.

We never killed The Horse. It's possible a neighbor or perhaps an automobile killed it. Whatever the case, that doe was smart enough to live at least 5-1/2 years in a heavily hunted county.

Three Success Stories

Although The Horse is now a legend in our hunting camp, dozens of old does did not escape us. In fact, my many seasons of hunting for old does have made me a much better buck hunter. First, mature does oftentimes exhibit buck-like behavior once they know they're being hunted. Second, by following mature does around the woods, I quickly learn the bedding areas, travel corridors and subtle terrain features that bucks will cruise during the rut. Knowledge like that gives me a definite leg up when October turns to November and bucks seemingly come out of the woodwork.

To outsmart mature does, you need to hunt fringe cover as the season progresses. The author bagged this Mississippi doe as it moved from a hardwood ridge toward a lowland swamp.

White-tailed does live in maternally related groups. These colonies are often complex and include individuals from up to seven social classes.

Two of the most memorable does that did not escape me were mature whitetails I killed while bowhunting. Both of these deer were hog-bodied does that lived in a chunk of big woods. I chased both of these does for several weeks during an early archery season. I finally caught up with one of them in mid-October. This doe had two fawns, and the three deer consistently bedded on a small oak ridge that sloped toward an overgrown pasture. After watching how deer used the pasture, I hung a stand and only hunted in the afternoon. During my first two sits, both fawns walked right underneath my stand. The doe eluded me, however, by taking alternate trails through the brush. I killed the doe after relocating my stand to a tree in the brush line. She was 4 years old and weighed 134 pounds field dressed (160 pounds on the hoof).

The hunt for the second monster doe was a bit more difficult. She also had two fawns and shared the same range as the first doe. This matriarch was also extremely wary. Starting in late October, the doe and fawns usually appeared on a wooded sidehill about an hour before sunset. They'd feed on acorns and woody browse, and eventually pass through the pasture on their way to a nearby crop field.

The doe constantly scanned the pasture for danger, and she often stood statuesquely while scent-checking the area. After many hours of observation, I determined that the only way I could kill this doe was to limit my hunts to days with a straight west or slight southwest wind. I also had to reposition my stand three times before finding a spot that put me in bow range of one of her preferred travel routes.

The hard work and careful observations paid off on the last day of our early archery season. Only a few minutes of shooting time remained when the doe stepped within 17 yards of my stand. My shot was true, and she ran just 40 yards before collapsing. That doe was 5-1/2 years old and field dressed at 137 pounds. I'm as proud of that deer as I am of any big bucks I've killed over the years.

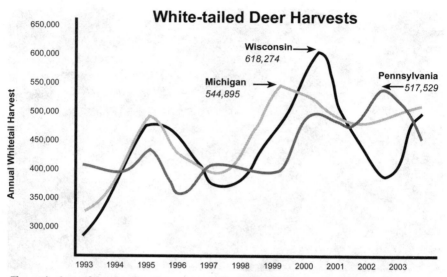

White-tailed Deer Harvests

Annual Whitetail Harvest

Wisconsin
618,274

Michigan →
544,895

Pennsylvania
← 517,529

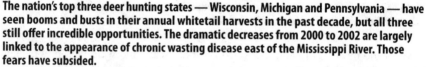

The nation's top three deer hunting states — Wisconsin, Michigan and Pennsylvania — have seen booms and busts in their annual whitetail harvests in the past decade, but all three still offer incredible opportunities. The dramatic decreases from 2000 to 2002 are largely linked to the appearance of chronic wasting disease east of the Mississippi River. Those fears have subsided.

As you can probably tell by now, I'm a deer hunter. Period. If it's got a white tail and snorts when it smells me, I instantly turn into that metabolic teen-ager who obsessively crossed off the days on his *Deer & Deer Hunting* calendar while waiting for hunting season. My third-most-memorable doe hunt took place more than a decade ago in the vast Chequamegon National Forest in northern Wisconsin. The area we hunted consisted of thousands of acres of unbroken wilderness. The forest – mostly mature with little understory – was (and still is) relatively poor deer habitat. Although deer densities in this area should be kept in the single digits for optimum herd health, years of baiting and supplemental feeding have artificially inflated densities in the upwards of 25 deer per square mile.

In the 1980s and early '90s, this forest attracted few hunters, which made it a fun place to hunt. A guy could literally hunt every minute of the state's 9-day gun season and never encounter another hunter in the woods. Deer sightings were equally rare, but success could be had if you did just a small amount of legwork. That's exactly what I did when I learned a small section of the forest had been clear-cut the previous winter. My buddy, Joe Peil, and I speed-scouted the area during an August fishing trip and learned that 6-month-old cut was already attracting heavy deer traffic. A tamarack swamp surrounded the cut – approximately 80 acres of mature aspen – to the south and a maple/oak ridge to the north. We spent maybe 45 minutes walking the perimeter and were pleasantly surprised when we jumped five deer, including two mammoth does. "Good enough for me," Joe said. "Guess we'll have to arm-wrestle to see who gets that spot," I added while pointing to a sentinel pine that grew at the edge of the forest about 75 yards away.

As we walked out, we noted how several heavily used deer trails bisected the property and headed for two huge brush piles in the middle of the cut. In hindsight, those brush piles were located on a small rise – a classic feature for most whitetail bedding areas. The cover and visibility allowed deer to rest while watching for danger in nearly all directions. The only blind spot was the tamarack swamp edge, as a slightly higher rise was sandwiched between the brush piles and woods' edge.

Despite this killer spot, Joe and I all but forgot about it when gun season rolled around. We hunted other promising spots and rationalized that we'd "save" the clearcut for still-hunting and/or drives later in the week. Yes, we did possess some youthful ignorance. It took several years, but we eventually learned that driving a young clearcut in wilderness country is a colossal waste of time. We spooked

The expansion of crossbows in regular archery seasons has provided new opportunities for hunters who otherwise wouldn't be able to hunt early seasons.

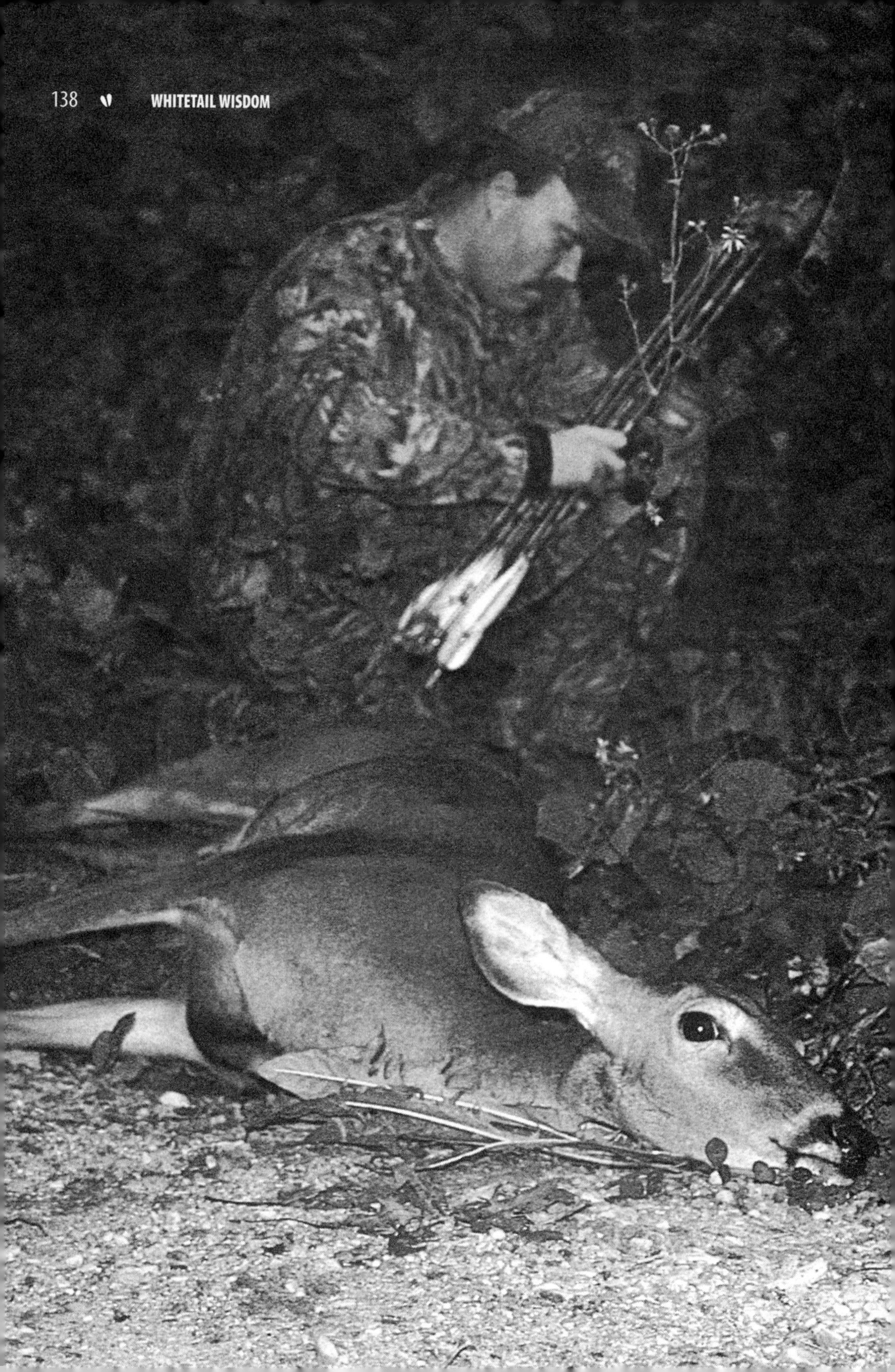

WHY HEAVY DOE HARVESTS ARE NECESSARY

❱❱ In 2004, the 42 states with notable whitetail populations were home to a total of 33 million deer. When you consider those same states had just 14.2 million active deer hunters, who claimed an annual harvest of 7.4 million deer, it's easy to see how and why we've come to a crossroads.

The aforementioned statistics show why deer herds are increasing, but that's only part of the story. Most professional biologists agree that 30 percent of any given deer herd must be killed each year to keep the numbers from spiraling upward. That's not happening in most parts of the country, and even states that are keeping up with "inflation" stand to lose much ground if they don't act quickly. Wisconsin – the nation's No. 1 deer hunting state – is a perfect example. Over the last five years, the Badger State was home to a herd that fluctuated between 1.6 million and 1.8 million deer. Hunters responded to the bounty by piling up a five-year average harvest of more than 467,000 deer annually. Impressive, but not nearly enough. To stand pat, hunters would have had to kill an average of 510,000 deer annually.

Making matters even worse, the chronic wasting disease scare of 2002/2003 resulted in the lowest harvest in nearly a decade. Mild winters and popular feeding and baiting practices resulted in deer-density spikes so high that some regions reported pre-hunt herds in excess of 100 deer per square mile of habitat. In an ideal world, those densities should be closer to 35 dpsm.

What's the answer? Heavy doe harvests, especially during early firearms seasons. Bowhunting is beneficial in urban environments, but it is certainly not the answer to meeting overall harvest quotas. Not to keep picking on Wisconsin, but archers there only kill, on average, 86,000 deer per year. That's just 18 percent of the state's overall annual harvest.

From the far North to the extreme South, whitetail herds are at all-time-high numbers. With ample doe tags, hunters can polish their skills in an incredibly short time frame.

more deer than we ever saw, and usually messed up our hunting prospects for the next several days. The still-hunting plan for this trip, however, worked and worked well.

It was the day after Thanksgiving when we finally re-visited the clearcut. The plan was simple: Joe, my dad and brother-in-law would take stands in the mature woods, while I still-hunted the clearcut. It was a cold, overcast day, and a 15 mph wind blew from the northwest. I knew if I played my cards right I could sneak to that sentinel pine without spooking any deer bedded near those brush piles. I certainly daydreamed about getting the drop on a buck, but would be lying if I didn't admit I was simply hoping to see one of those square-jawed does.

It took me about an hour to cover a few hundred yards. By the time I reached the pine, I realized the surrounding brush and aspen regrowth would make it impossible to crest the sidehill without being heard or seen. So, instead of taking the direct route, I decided to go for it by slipping around the corner and stalking straight for the brush piles. After all, I had a scoped .30-06.

The stalk was on. I pushed forward one premeditated step at a time. After a few tense moments, I spied movement near the brush piles. Two huge does rose from their beds. They weren't spooked, but they knew I was getting closer. That's all I needed, as I slowly sunk to one knee and steadied the crosshairs on the largest doe's shoulder blade. At the sound of the shot, she dropped in her tracks. We were exhausted by the time we pulled that doe back to camp, but the camaraderie and fried venison tenderloins that followed placed this hunt near the top of my list for most-cherished hunting memories.

When it comes to herd management, gun-hunters are the grunts who do the lion's share of population control. That's why it's important for all hunters to unite and fight to keep gun-hunting options open.

In 2004, the 42 states with notable whitetail populations were home to a total of 33 million deer.

HOW TO MATCH WITS WITH A MATRIARCH

The hunter who pays close attention to details can enjoy immediate success on big does by following these guidelines:

❧ **Dedicate two to three days to scouting a preferred food source.** Observe and note deer behavior at the same time every morning and/or evening. Pinpoint the doe or does you want to harvest. Use binoculars and identify the single-most used trail or entry point leading to the food source.

❧ **Hang a tree stand or place a ground blind within shooting range of the trail.** Be sure to groom your ambush locations at least three full days before your first hunt. The best location will provide downwind shooting opportunities to the main trail, plus one or two secondary trails.

❧ **Do not enter the hunting area during peak activity times, and keep pruning activity to a minimum.** Strive for stand locations that provide natural shooting lanes. Mature does will easily pinpoint your stand if you carelessly cut limbs, clear brush or erect stands that stick out like sore thumbs.

❧ **Do not hunt the stand or blind unless wind conditions are favorable.** This rule isn't as hard and fast if your mission is to harvest any antlerless deer. However, you will most likely ruin your chances of outsmarting an old doe if you risk it and hunt during less-than-ideal conditions. Mature does rarely make the same mistake twice.

❧ **Do not shoot the first deer you see ... unless it's the big doe!** Early season deer activity is highly predictable. Invariably, a buck fawn or yearling doe will be the first deer to appear at a food source. Old does can appear at any time, but they are usually tardy. Be patient, and you'll greatly improve your odds of outsmarting the oldest doe of a large doe group.

Defining the Classes

White-tailed does live in maternally related groups. According to researchers, these colonies are often complex and include individuals from up to seven social classes. The first three categories include fawns, yearlings and/or first-time mothers. Then come the dispersers, which are second-time mothers. These deer usually make up new homes a quarter-mile or more from their birth locations. The final categories include three levels of matriarchs and, finally, seniors. Matriarchs are prime-age does ranging from 4 to 10 years old. A doe doesn't classify for senior status until she reaches age 12. A hunter would have a better chance at getting hit by lightning or possibly winning the Megabucks lottery than he would of killing a senior-class doe.

Hunters who kill matriarchs provide the greatest service to deer management programs. "Matriarchs represent the epitome of health and physical fitness," said John Ozoga, the legendary deer researcher from Munising, Mich. "They are the survivors, the machines that permit a population to grow at a maximum rate."

On the other hand, hunters shouldn't become bent on only hunting for mature does. As far as herd management is concerned, any doe is a good doe to take off the landscape and into your freezer. Texas biologist Bob Zaiglin explained it best when he said "Hunters should refrain from using complicated criteria when shooting antlerless deer, because does respond quickly to increased hunting pressure. Achieving antlerless harvest objectives is much easier when such seasons open, because hunter success is high, thus fewer hunters are required to meet harvest quotas."

"Naive, easy-to-hunt does quickly become wily," Zaiglin continued. "This is one reason hunters see relatively few does on well-managed areas. Does adapt to hunting

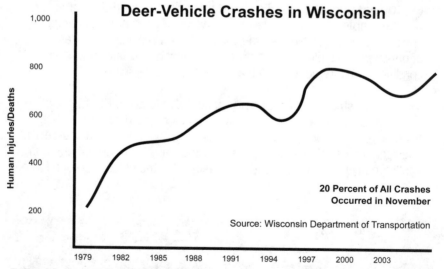

Deer-Vehicle Crashes in Wisconsin

Human Injuries/Deaths

1,000 / 800 / 600 / 400 / 200

20 Percent of All Crashes Occurred in November

Source: Wisconsin Department of Transportation

1979 1982 1985 1988 1991 1994 1997 2000 2003

Today's burgeoning deer herds have provided more than just increased hunting opportunities. With the sobering information of increased automobile collisions, resulting in human injuries and deaths, hunters should feel obligated to fill as many doe tags as possible each and every hunting season.

pressure and rely on their inherent survival techniques. And if you think bucks are the smartest deer in the woods, you haven't matched wits with an old doe."

Proven Tactics

Find a productive food source, and you'll find antlerless deer. However, mature does – like mature bucks – aren't pushovers. Field edges, water sources, food plots and orchards are great spots to kill big does during the early archery season, but these spots quickly dry up when the older deer start feeling the pressure.

To outsmart mature does, you need to hunt fringe cover as the season progresses. My most productive stands are essentially staging areas – patches of thick cover adjacent to feeding areas. My best spot is a select-cut pine forest that abuts a clover field. The varying stages of regrowth provide fantastic cover and good hunting spots. Afternoon hunting is usually best in these types of areas, because deer congregate in the thicker cover, seemingly waiting for darkness to approach so they can enter the field. Some of these areas might only be an acre or so in size, but older does seek them and use them routinely.

Field hunting is frustrating because does use fields as open-area feeding havens throughout summer. They enter the fields from positions that allow them to scan for danger well in advance, and they oftentimes just pause at the woods' edge and then jog or sprint until they're 50 to 75 yards into the field. I believe this behavior indicates they instinctively know they're safer when they can see for long distances in every direction.

Such wary deer are hard to kill, but several tactics help improve a hunter's odds.

If you're a seasoned doe hunter, you've probably killed your share of buck fawns. Mistakes happen and, in fact, are sometimes unavoidable.

One tactic I use is to hang a stand so it overlooks a well-used trail 20 to 50 yards inside the woods. Place the stand 10 to 15 yards off the primary trail. The most productive stands are those that provide shooting coverage to a main trail as well as one or more secondary trails. Once pressured, mature does often adopt buck-like behavior in that they'll "bring up the rear," allowing younger deer – typically fawns – to enter food sources on primary trails, while they hang back and enter from secondary trails.

Another proven tactic involves glassing the food source throughout the off-season and learning the exact spots where deer enter it. Next, you need to find a stand location that's within shooting distance of the entrance route and one that takes advantage of prevailing wind currents. Hang stands well in advance of the first hunt, and only hunt the spot when the wind is perfect. Young deer might make repeated mistakes, but older does will not. As a result, it's crucial to have two or three backup stands to cover various wind conditions. When hunting mature does at field edges, bowhunters need to be on constant alert. When a big doe steps into the field, the hunter usually needs to whistle or bleat with his mouth to get the deer to stop before she trots toward the field's "safety zone."

Remember, devising tactics to outsmart individual deer doesn't need to be exhausting. With some planning and legwork, hunters can quickly assess how doe groups use the terrain. Draw maps for noting terrain features and deer sign. Major runways are easy to find, and they can tell you a lot about deer movements. For example, a runway that connects different cover types, such as oak forests and pine thickets, likely indicates preferred feeding and bedding areas. However, don't be fooled into believing a well-used deer trail is your ticket to a filled tag. To outsmart wise, old does, use main runways as starting points, and scout the area for parallel trails. In fact, these are the types of trails where hunters are most likely to connect on first- or second-time sits in farm country.

On the other hand, big-woods does are much harder to kill. When targeting matriarchs in vast forests, hunters are best served to hunt oak ridges and swamp bottlenecks early in the archery season and travel corridors and clearcuts during the firearms season and late bow season. Big-woods hunting requires much more scouting and trial-and-error hunting. When targeting wilderness areas, I've found that morning hunts near bedding areas are more productive than afternoon hunts.

Unfortunately, with the increasing popularity of baiting in many Northern states, hunting deer one-on-one has become a bit more difficult in recent years. I hunted Wisconsin's vast national forests until baiting became so bad that many hunters "squatted" on certain areas. The situation came to a head in the mid-1990s when a guy approached within 150 yards of me, stopped and stared me down with his arms crossed. He just stood there for 10 minutes until I decided to confront him. As I walked toward him, a huge bait pile came into view. "This is my spot," he said. I told him, "No, this is public land, and I have a right to hunt here the same as you. ... But I won't hunt here now." Of course, that didn't faze him. He stayed put over his illegal bait pile and killed a spike buck that afternoon. With such intense hunting pressure like that, you can imagine how difficult it was to hunt "the old fashioned way." Needless to say, I found new forests in which to chase wily old does.

UNDERSTANDING BUCK-FAWN BIOLOGY

To understand buck-fawn harvest dynamics, you first need to understand natural buck-fawn birth and mortality rates. According to Bill Mytton, Wisconsin's chief deer ecologist, does usually give birth to more buck fawns than doe fawns, and those buck fawns typically die – from various natural causes – at a higher rate than doe fawns. Therefore, "sparing" them during hunting season accomplishes little.

When antlerless-season critics are faced with harvest figures showing buck-fawn kills are constant and make up a relatively small percentage of the overall harvest, they commonly contest that such figures gloss over the fact many of those bucks were killed in relatively small areas, resulting in "holes" in buck ranges. However, scientific study of yearling buck dispersal behavior disproves this argument.

According to researchers, domination by female relatives causes most bucks to disperse from their birth range by age 1. This prevents bucks from eventually breeding their mothers and sisters. What's more, in studies conducted in Minnesota, Michigan, Illinois and Georgia, yearling bucks dispersed 3 miles to 100 miles, depending on habitat quality, deer densities and herd structures. Regardless of the distance, dispersal prevents "empty spots" in buck range.

Yet another study, led by Missouri biologist Lonnie Hansen, showed that 70 percent of all bucks dispersed from their birth range by the time they were 18 months old. Two regions were studied, and dispersal distances averaged 9 miles and 24 miles, respectively.

Most professional biologists agree that 30 percent of any given deer herd must be killed each year to keep the numbers from spiraling upward. With that in mind, hunters with unfilled antlerless tags should never pass up a chance at a mature doe.

Be Aware of Buck Fawns

If you're a seasoned doe hunter, you've probably killed your share of buck fawns. Mistakes happen and, in fact, are sometimes unavoidable. Some buck fawns, especially in Northern locales, can weigh 100 pounds or more on the hoof.

One of the best examples of an honest mistake that I've witnessed happened in 1995 when I shared a bowhunt at the northeast Wisconsin home of *Deer & Deer Hunting* associate publisher Brad Rucks and a Southern hunter whom I have always considered a living legend. This gentleman had more deer hunting experience in his left little finger than Rucks and I had combined. His experience, however, was gained mostly in the South, and he was absolutely stunned when he learned the "huge doe" he shot with his recurve that afternoon wound up being an 80-pound button buck. "I don't know what to say, Brad," the bowhunter said. "Where I come from, this would be a monster doe."

I've taken my share of ribbing over the years, too. In fact, I've killed more than 125 deer in my life, and 13 of them have been buck fawns. However, of those fawns, at least half of them sported buttons so small that they couldn't be detected without hands-on inspection. When hunting antlerless deer, I prefer to shoot any doe – adult or fawn – when given the choice. Ask any biologist, and they'll tell you it's imperative to shoot fawns, because a healthy herd is one that has an even distribution of deer from all age classes.

"Shooting doe fawns makes biological sense, especially on Northern range, because fawns represent the herd's most numerous single age class," Ozoga said. "Furthermore, doe fawns contribute little or nothing toward reproduction the next year."

As you can tell, I'll never run for the roof if I accidentally kill a buck fawn. My attitude on this topic stems largely from the fact that I live and hunt in an area that routinely has a pre-hunt population of more than 70 deer per square mile. A healthy density would be closer to 30 dpsm. Therefore, any mouth out of the food chain helps management goals and improves the habitat.

Head size and shape is the most reliable method for distinguishing an adult doe from a buck fawn. Adults have long muzzles, and older does have square, blocky foreheads. Most fawns have short ears, pug-nosed muzzles and small, round heads.

Again, don't be ashamed if you make a mistake. According to data compiled by the Quality Deer Management Association, deer densities are above goals in most parts of the country. Scientific studies have shown that buck fawns typically account for less than 25 percent of annual antlerless harvests. The bottom line: Killing buck fawns is a necessary evil to accomplishing long-term herd-management goals.

Step 9
Become A Buck Hunter

White-tailed deer are creatures of habit. If they weren't, hunters would never see them – and put themselves in position to kill deer – with such regularity. After all, we base nearly all of our scouting and hunting decisions on where deer have been. Trails, rubs, scrapes and distinct browse lines allow hunters to pattern deer to some degree. Although observations point us in general areas for improved deer sightings, can big, mature bucks really be patterned to the extent that so many experts have claimed over the years? I'd answer that question with a qualified "yes." However, it requires much prefacing. More on that in a moment.

To become a buck hunter, you must make the pledge to seriously study deer and deer behavior. There's little luck involved. There's a reason why this chapter is buried near the end of this book. The most successful buck hunters in North America didn't earn their stripes overnight. They were deer hunters first and foremost and eventually turned the corner. Too many young hunters watch the Outdoor Channel and popular hunting videos and think they can achieve big-buck stardom by studying buck sign and hunting hard through the rut. And, truth be told, today's burgeoning herds and a shift toward quality deer management has helped some of these upstarts taste occasional success. To do it consistently – especially on big deer – requires many seasons of trial and error.

Keep an Open Mind

I will never claim to have all – or even one-half – of the answers when it comes to hunting white-tailed deer. Each deer is different, as is each situation. Although general patterns emerge, deer from different parts of the country seemingly possess regional traits.

While earning my stripes as a bowhunter, I fell hook-line-and-sinker the first time an old-timer described the "October lull." According to him, a hunter might as well put his bow and arrows away and pull out the grouse gun when September gives way to autumn's most glorious month. He claimed deer all but went nocturnal during "leaf off," typically the first two weeks of October in my home state of Wisconsin. After dozens of deerless days in the field, I concluded that old guy knew what he was talking about. It's funny how such silly absolutes have their way of becoming hard-and-fast rules among hunting's general population.

My opinion changed in the mid-1990s when I was fortunate enough to share camps with legendary hunters like Charles Alsheimer of New York, Gary Clancy of Minnesota, John Trout Jr. of Indiana and Greg Miller of Wisconsin. All of these guys were studying and tagging big whitetails before I was even born, and, to a man, all four will say the so-called October lull is more myth than mystery. That's not to say they don't believe deer undergo drastic changes from their early season habits. However, all four will tell you – off the record – that too much hype is placed on what is otherwise an extremely fun time to hunt.

Alsheimer's words have always spoken volumes. In fact, if I hadn't hung on his every word, I'd probably still be chasing grouse and woodcock during mid-October.

◀ **Decoying is a fantastic rut-time tactic, but it usually works best when hunting areas with low deer densities and properties with relatively equal buck-to-doe ratios.**

Instead, I've collected October-lull whitetails by merely studying my hunting land more closely during every hunt. I've also learned a few strategies that have helped me better estimate what deer will do, and when they will do it.

October success on mature whitetails hinges on three pieces of information: the precise locations of preferred bedding areas, travel routes and food sources. Many diehard buck hunters insist on memorizing aerial maps and spending countless post-season hours scouting their land. These guys are usually very successful, and they work extremely hard – almost to a point of unhealthy obsession – to tag monster bucks every year. I'm not one of these guys. I prefer to enjoy my time afield, even if that means hunting distant stands on occasion just to observe how

You'll start tagging more bucks if you keep an open mind and stop believing all the old-time myths that state deer "always do this," or "always do that."

Deer don't wear wristwatches. They can be outsmarted at any time of the day at any time of the season.

deer use the property. Watching deer – rather than guessing what they'll do – often reveals dozens of unpredictable nuances in topography and deer behavior.

To be successful in October, hunters need to possess good memories – or take precise notes – on how deer on their property eat, sleep and travel. These variables obviously can change drastically from year to year, but once you figure them out, you'll wonder why it took you so long.

Consider a 9-point buck I killed a few years ago as a good example of how things can fall together quickly. This hunt took place on a property I started hunting in the late 1990s. It was my fourth year of hunting the property, and – despite the fortune of taking many does during the bow and gun seasons – bucks were routinely giving me the slip. The tide turned when I spent several weeks hunting each corner of the property. The mission was simple: Take a climbing stand to predetermined sites, hunt each spot for a full morning and afternoon, then move on to the next spot. However, instead of just watching deer, I intently studied their every move – what types of deer showed up; when they showed; what trails they used; how they used them; what they ate; and how they entered nearby fields.

I managed to fill many doe tags in the process, but this shotgun approach provided invaluable insights into how bucks used the property. After compiling my notes, I pinpointed two specific areas where bucks routinely showed up. From there, it took just a half-day of December scouting to determine both spots were relatively close to prime bedding areas. The better of the two spots featured a rub line from that fall and old rubs from the previous year. I immediately picked out a stand site and returned in July to hang my stand. I hunted the stand twice during September's early bow season and saw a few bucks, but didn't receive a shot opportunity. I didn't panic; I knew this stand would eventually produce because it was literally at the doorstep of a fantastic bedding area. My lucky day came on Oct. 5.

There's nothing wrong with holding out for Mr. Big, but be forewarned that you might go for several seasons without filling a buck tag.

It was a muggy, misty afternoon when I climbed to my stand. This wasn't the most exciting hunt I've ever had. In fact, it was probably one of the most boring! Nothing was moving, and aspen leaves were already falling from the trees. The stand faced the bedding area – a thick pine grove – and a lush alfalfa field to the west had been the preferred feeding area for about two weeks. I had been perched in my stand for nearly four hours when the sun finally dipped below the tree line. That's when I saw him – a beautiful 9-pointer still carrying crimson highlights on his neck and forehead. He bobbed and weaved through the pines, then walked straight for the corner of the field. It was the first deer I saw that day, but that didn't matter, because he was definitely one I wanted to shoot. The buck took the same route that I had watched many of the other deer use during previous sits from distant spots. He had no clue I was there, and he soon walked to the base of my tree.

Successful buck-hunters are those guys who never give up and constantly add new tactics to their overall approach.

The buck was cautious but not overly alert. In fact, he was so at ease with his surroundings that he licked the rungs of my steel ladder. My all-encompassing scent-free approach obviously helped with that, but before this particular hunt I doused my rubber boots with Carbon Blast spray from Robinson Labs. To this day, I swear that is the only reason why that buck hung around so long. How long? Well, he stood there for exactly eight minutes ... I know, because I timed him! You can imagine how hard my heart was beating as I stared straight down through the mesh grate platform while waiting for him to make his next move. He did, eventually, by walking perfectly into a shooting lane. He stopped at 12 yards and quartered away. My arrow went through him so fast that I never heard it make contact. The buck ran about 75 yards before collapsing.

The scene at the gas station was quite amusing. Drenched with sweat from dragging my buck across the alfalfa field, I headed for the cooler, grabbed a bottle of Coke and then walked toward the cashier. Another guy, who was donning a camouflage cap, was paying for his gasoline. "Out there bowhunting, huh?" he asked. "I don't waste my time during the lull," he said. "I wait till the rut."

"Yeah, it's pretty tough," I replied while smiling and looking toward the cashier. "Oh, by the way, I have a buck to register." I couldn't help but feel a tad smug as I watched the other hunter's jaw nearly drop to the counter.

HOW TO BECOME A BUCK HUNTER

❧   **Keep an open mind.** Stop believing all the old-time myths, and you'll start tagging more bucks. The best time for killing a hog-bodied buck isn't when the moon is full or waxing or waning. It isn't during the first week of early archery season when bucks are still in bachelor groups, and it isn't when when October gives way to November. The best time to kill a hog-bodied buck is after you've done enough scouting to learn where deer travel and when you've perched your scent-free body and gear in a tree that he decides to walk by on a given day. Deer don't wear wristwatches. They can be outsmarted at any time of the day at any time of the season. The morning you talk yourself out of going hunting could be the morning when that buck you've been after makes a huge rub within spitting distance of your tree stand.

❧   **Shrug off bad advice.** Leave words like *never* and *always* out of your deer hunting vocabulary. Above all, don't be talked out of going to the woods. Phrases like "October lull" and "nocturnal bucks" are excuses for guys who get their butts kicked and don't want to admit it. The best old-timer absolute advice I've ever heard is, "You'll never kill a deer if you stay in bed all morning."

❧   **Read and understand the signs.** Bucks make rubs and scrapes to provide visual and olfactory signposts for other deer, but deer hunters overrate rubs. Although it's true that mature bucks living on low-density habitat can be outsmarted along well-defined rub lines, time-strapped hunters are best served by using rubs as starting points for scouting forays. After locating clusters of rubs, dissect the immediate hunting area and look for travel corridors and pinch points that lead to and from bedding and feeding areas. In that regard, rubs are better than scrapes for pinpointing ambush sites, because scrapes are often random and don't always include a licking branch.

❧   **Become a trail wizard.** Realize that well-worn deer trails aren't sure-fire tickets to success. Instead of hastily popping up a stand that overlooks a trail, dissect the area and learn how deer use the trail and where it leads in all directions. A few minutes of forethought will reveal bedding and feeding areas. These spots provide better clues as to where to hang stands and how to hunt the area when targeting mature deer vs. just any deer.

❧   **Set realistic goals.** The guys on TV and in the magazines kill big bucks – oftentimes several in one season – for a good reason: They have great places to hunt. There's nothing wrong with dreaming about wrapping your tag on Ol' Mossyhorns, but don't let such aspirations desensitize you to that perfectly fine 100-inch buck that's the king of your 40-acre woodlot.

Rubs and Scrapes

The whitetail's most visible rut-time signs also have spawned deep-rooted myths. Count, if you can, how many times you've heard someone say, "Small rubs always equal small deer. You have to find big rubs to find big deer." What's the count? Probably dozens, right? Unfortunately, that blanket statement is yet another whitetail myth.

Although big rubs are a good indicator that a big deer is roaming the countryside, sign alone does not indicate if, or how many, big deer frequent a property. Well-developed yearlings and average-sized 2-year-old bucks can leave calf-sized rubs. These rubs, however, are usually sparse. Rub lines that feature consistently large rubs are good indicators you're dealing with a mature buck.

A mature big-woods buck I killed in 2002 made nothing but small, sapling-sized rubs across his home territory. I knew the buck was there, and, frankly, was surprised by the lack of sign. I didn't realize why until after I killed him. He weighed 245 pounds on the hoof and sported a Pope-and-Young-class rack, but his beam tips curved so far inward that they nearly touched. When he rubbed, he either had to choose a 2-inch sapling, or rub the trees with the sides of his rack.

Rubs are certainly exciting to a deer hunter, but they're highly unreliable for forecasting buck movement ... unless concentrated in a well-defined line in a classic travel corridor. Rubs basically tell you where a buck has been, and close study can reveal what direction he was traveling when he made them. When hunting, let rubs confirm you've selected a good piece of terrain. Don't make the mistake of merely placing a stand within shooting distance of a rub or two. Instead, dissect the area and key off of trails, corners and areas where dense cover overlaps with more open areas.

My views on scrapes and scrape hunting are similar to those on rubs, but I place less faith in active scrapes during the rut. The few scrapes that are worth hunting are those located inside the woods and include an active licking branch. I've wasted many hours hunting over field-side scrapes. Sure, I saw a few deer, even killed some does and young bucks over them; but field scrapes are not worth the effort, because they're invariably made and revisited under the cover of darkness.

Licking branches are crucial because they serve as a communication hub for every deer in the area. In the absence of real licking branches, hunters can literally take matters into their own hands and create whitetail hotspots. Merely find a well-used trail or crossing and break a stout branch so it hangs at chest level. Or, better yet, saw off a branch and use wire or a plastic cinch tie to anchor it to another low-hanging branch. This tactic can be taken one step further by creating a mock scrape, but it's not necessary. If you're careful not to contaminate the branch with human scent, deer will start using it as a licking branch. Charles Alsheimer taught me this trick when I visited his western New York farm in 1998, and I've experienced incredible success with it ever since. Once deer start using a licking branch, they show up like clockwork when they're passing through an area. Bucks are typically the only deer that will urinate in the scrape, but does and fawns invariably stop and use the licking branch.

After locating clusters of rubs, dissect the immediate hunting area and look for travel corridors and pinch points that lead to and from bedding and feeding areas.

Can human urine be effective in mock scrapes? Most definitely. The key, however, is moderation. This is another trick that Alsheimer has perfected. After creating a mock scrape, he makes sure the ground is completely void of all leaves and debris, and then urinates directly into the soil for maybe 15 seconds. The resulting ammonia reaction is similar to that of deer urine. In fact, some hunters claim that they get the same results by using regular household ammonia. That's quite possible, because urine is basically the same thing after it comes in contact with air and soil.

The urination tactic is effective in prompting bucks to approach the scrapes, smell the ground and feverishly re-work them. Be warned: This tactic doesn't work all the time. I have spooked deer from scrapes that I've urinated into, but I attribute most of those failures to accidentally urinating on nearby leaves or grass. Although urinating in a scrape might sound a bit over the top to some hunters, trust me, it's a cheap and effective way of outsmarting white-tailed bucks.

Become a Trail Wizard

The advent of scouting cameras has taken buck hunting to new levels and provides hunters with in-depth insights into deer behavior. In fact, many high-profile hunters use these cameras to unravel the secrets behind trail-use trends.

Mature bucks are complex creatures, and no two are the same. However, big bucks show some similarities when using well-worn game trails. First, older bucks tend to

The best part about those good, old days was that antler size was inconsequential.

The advent of scouting cameras has taken buck hunting to new levels and provides hunters with in-depth insights into deer behavior.

stay on main trails less than doe groups and young bucks. They often skirt major runways, cut corners and use parallel routes. Why they do this is poorly understood, but it's possible they're merely more cautious and less prone to "trust" the instincts of other deer. On the other hand, older bucks might just be more adaptable because they probably have encountered more pressure in hunted environments. A good example of how bucks use trails and cover was shown many years ago during a scientific study by a team of Illinois biologists led by Charles Nixon. According to the researchers, heavily pressured mature bucks often use obscure trails to enter thick cover, and they will remain in cover for days without moving. The most extreme case featured one mature buck that sought refuge in a cornfield and stayed there for nearly an entire month. A deer like that would be nearly impossible to hunt, but this example shows how important it is to control human scent and hunter presence on smaller properties when your goal is to hunt older bucks.

Even on sparsely pressured land, mature bucks have a comfort zone that only they know. Another key to targeting these deer involves knowing how to pinpoint subtle changes in the landscape and predict how bucks use them in their daily travels. For example, let's say your land consists of a 3-year-old pine clearcut bordering mature oaks and a thick creek bottom. A well-worn deer trail winds through the clearcut and pops out into the oak about 100 yards from the stream. There's nothing wrong with popping up a stand at the intersection, and, in fact, it would be a great ambush site to kill does or younger bucks during the early season. Could you kill a mature buck there? Certainly, since anything is possible. However, closer inspection of the area might reveal secondary trails and, most likely, one or more cut-off trails angling toward the oaks and/or creek bottom. Stand sites in those areas might be slim and more difficult to access. They might even result in fewer deer sightings. However, it's a good bet those out-of-the-way spots will produce mature-buck sightings, especially during the rut. Older bucks are not only smart; they're often lazy. If a shortcut means shaving 50 yards off their final destination, they almost always take such routes.

Remember, don't be fooled into thinking well worn trails will always result in many deer sightings. The opposite is often true, especially in big-woods environments, because such trails are typically nighttime routes. Trails are merely highways from bedding to feeding areas. There's nothing wrong with getting excited about finding one of these thoroughfares, but it's important to view a gem of a trail as the beginning piece to a puzzle containing many pieces. Then, ask yourself lots of questions. Which direction are deer primarily traveling? Where's the major food source? What is it? Is it still viable, or did it dry up weeks ago? Where's the bedding area? How can I access a potential stand site without spooking bedded deer? The most important questions, however, should deal with predominant wind directions and morning/ evening thermals. This sounds like a lot of work, but it really isn't, especially with a few seasons of experience under your belt. The really good hunters are those who automatically click off the questions and answers as they scout new areas or hunt them "on the fly" for the first time.

Fantasy vs. Reality

We all love watching those deer hunting videos and TV shows where the semi-famous hunter whacks a mature buck at point-blank range. The following segment

Realistic goal setting is the first step to becoming a buck hunter.

typically shows the same hunter with two or three sets of sheds from the same buck. "Yep, this ol' Mossy Horns," the hunter will say. "We've captured him on scouting cameras since he was a yearling. This is proof of how big a buck can grow if you pass him up when he's young."

Such examples are rarely fabricated, and the advice is sound, but too many everyday hunters take it as gospel. Trophy buck management works "like in the movies" if everyone in your camp is on board and if you control enough quality habitat to hold deer. That's why realistic goal setting is the first step to becoming a buck hunter. Defining what is realistic is tough, because it involves myriad factors. I'll give it a shot anyway.

Even the most prime piece of deer hunting land shouldn't be home to more than 35 deer per square mile. So, if you own or control 320 acres, the habitat would provide enough quality food for 17 deer. That means you'd have about nine bucks, including two or three that are 3 years old or older. Therefore, under a strict trophy-hunting program, your hunting group would be lucky to fill three buck tags in one season. Complicating these scenarios even further is the fact that researchers have proven that landowners cannot "stockpile" bucks. Just because you pass them up this year, doesn't mean they'll be around next season. Most bucks disperse twice by the time they're 2 years old. What invariably happens is that you wind up growing deer for your neighbors to shoot.

That example emphasizes a need for realistic goal setting for harvest strategies. There's nothing wrong with holding out for Mr. Big, but be forewarned that you might go several seasons without filling a buck tag. Hunters who show such restraint and satisfy their venison needs by filling doe tags are truly a notch above the rest of the heap.

I hate it when people refer to deer hunting as a sport. It's a pastime – an activity that's been in our blood since Day 1. Sports are about numbers, and many of today's buck hunters love to throw them around in the form of antler scores. The popular Boone and Crockett and Pope and Young scoring systems are useful in quantifying the size of a buck, and that's the only reason why I use them in daily conversations with hunters. However, scores can help hunters understand what to expect from their land. The following chart is a general buck-hunting guide for landowners in most parts of whitetail country (excluding Texas, the Deep South and extreme Northeast):

Parcel Size	Realistic Antler Score	Buck's Age
Less than 40 acres	50 inches	1 year
40 to 100 acres	100 inches	2 years
100 to 149 acres	120 inches	3 years
150 acres or more	140 inches	4-plus years

This chart should not be interpreted as an endorsement of state-mandated antler restrictions. Scientific research has proven that state-mandated restrictions do little to improve the overall health and well-being of deer herds. Pennsylvania has shown that it can work in micromanaging some tracts when coupled with heavy doe harvests.

Just months after learning he had cancer, the author's father bagged his first archery buck. The experience – not the buck's rack – made for a memorable season.

The greater point, however, is that restrictions mostly divide hunters by invoking the will of big-buck hunters on meat hunters and other hunters who find equal enjoyment out of harvesting any legal buck. To me, each hunt and each deer is different. In fact, my most memorable hunts are those in which I've killed does and small bucks, and even hunts when I didn't unleash an arrow or fire a bullet. Granted, meat hunters would be best served to target as many does as possible, but it goes deeper than that. How many people do you know that proudly display their forks, 6-pointers and small 8-point racks in their homes, garages and sheds? I know a lot of them.

How to handle inexperienced hunters is another point that gets lost in the antler-restriction debate. Proponents say rookies should be forced to play by the same rules as everyone else. Some make comparisons to the legal age requirements for drinking alcohol or driving a car. Letting rookies shoot small bucks is a bit more complicated. It doesn't have to do with "just killing something." Deer hunting is an evolutionary process. To an inexperienced hunter, a small 6-pointer walking through the woods is the equivalent of the Hansen Buck. Asking them to pass up small bucks is a sure recipe for turning them off to hunting before they get thoroughly hooked. In a way, it's a lot like today's catch-and-release mentality in fishing. The same guys who preach "Throw 'em all back" are the same ones who have photo albums stacked with images from 20 years ago that show them holding sagging stringers of bass, pike and walleyes. It's a classic case of "Do as I say, not as I did."

My strong feelings on this subject probably stem from the fact that I've seen many sons and daughters of avid hunters who have either dropped out of hunting altogether or never really embraced it from the start. I think they burn out quickly because they become much like the Little Leaguer whose dad pushes him so hard that he loses his love for the game.

One last point: If your camp or hunting club does have antler restrictions, consider including an exception for non-rookies as well. Every time I talk about antler restrictions, I think about my best friend, Joe, a guy I've known since high school. Whereas Joe lives and works near a big city, I'm usually never more than 10 minutes from my favorite tree stand. Joe is a deer fanatic and loves to hunt as much as I do, but his job as a corporate accounting manager (and the father of two young boys) doesn't provide him with much free time. His bow- and gun-hunting seasons are limited to a few days each year. What's more, most of his hunting takes place on public land. He has killed some antlerless deer over the years, but buck sightings have been relatively few and far between.

When Joe visits our home, I work hard to get him access to some small private parcels I hunt. All of these properties are home to some dandy bucks, but I wouldn't for a moment think of imposing an antler restriction on him. The invitation is always the same, "Take any deer you want."

When Joe visited in November 2003, he took his climbing stand to his favorite spot. Pouring rain and dense fog couldn't keep him out of the woods that day, and at about 8 a.m., he called in after killing a yearling 6-pointer. It was his first antlered buck in more than 15 years. I don't know who was happier – Joe or me – but I do know this: No silly antler restrictions were going to come between two friends and one incredibly magical moment.

... And Don't Obsess About Antler Scores

The spark that ignited my passion for whitetails struck me sometime in the late 1970s. Although my first deer hunt was a few years off, I became enamored with the hunt, especially successful ones. The best day of the year was the Sunday after Thanksgiving. That's when my dad and brothers returned from deer camp. Dad would always pull into the driveway with his truck loaded with hunting clothes, a freshly cut Christmas tree, and one, or sometimes two, frozen deer carcasses.

The defining moment of my early deer hunting education came one year when they returned with an 8-point buck. Well, we called it an 8-pointer, but it was something more like a 5-1/2-pointer because it had several tines broken from fighting. That was the beauty of deer hunting back then. Nobody ever thought about putting a tape measure to the antlers of a buck. Don't get me wrong; antlers captured as much attention then as they do today, but the translations were vastly different. A 6-pointer was an "ordinary" buck, while an 8-pointer was a "good" buck. The 10-pointers were really special. Anything more than that was usually killed by someone else at some other distant camp. A 12-, 14- or 16-pointer was like Snuffalupagus of Sesame Street – you heard a lot about them, but you never, ever saw one for yourself.

The best part about those good, old days was that antler size was inconsequential. An 8-pointer was an 8-pointer; it didn't matter if it had an 8-inch spread or an 18-inch spread. After gun season, the guys returned to their dart and bowling leagues and swapped reports with their buddies. I remember one guy who could sum up his camp's season in one sentence: "Yep, we got nine deer, Danny. Nine of 'em! Two 10-poin'ers, tree 8-poin'ers, a little 6 and tree big does." That was it. No lengthy discussions on mass measurements or net scores. No mentions of brow tines or

To become a successful buck hunter, you must make the pledge to seriously study deer behavior.

sticker points. No typical this or nontypical that. Guys simply didn't care. Antlers were cool to look at, but they weren't worshipped like they are today. To them, hunting was about meat acquisition and camp camaraderie.

It's hard for me to stand on my soap box and spout off on the evils of antler worship, because I appreciate big bucks as much as the next guy. My point in all of this is to emphasize how much I believe in staying true to your roots. My passion for deer hunting has allowed me to hone my skills to the point where I can kill a big buck every now and then. However, I believe enjoying the hunt, savoring the venison and making memories with family and friends should always come first. The day I allow antler obsessions to overpower my innocent appreciation for all things wild is the day I want to be escorted out of the woods.

The best example of innocent appreciation comes from a true story that happened in my camp a few years ago. Bear with me if you've already heard this one, because I've repeated it a thousand times!

It was opening day of gun season, and my brother Ken killed a huge 10-pointer. He had gone 20 years without killing a deer, but this one was one to remember because it laid claim to being the biggest deer ever killed by anyone in our family. The excitement generated by that buck spread like wildfire throughout our family, and by the end of the week, everyone in town knew about it. The best moment came when our gang was gathered in my backyard, and everyone was taking photos of Kenny with his buck. Everyone stood alert and wide-eyed, and it was cold enough to see puffs of air exiting their excited mouths.

"Gosh, this rack is huge," someone said while closely admiring Kenny's buck. "What does it score?" it didn't take but a moment for someone else to reply. "Who cares?"

Step 10
Shoot Like A Pro

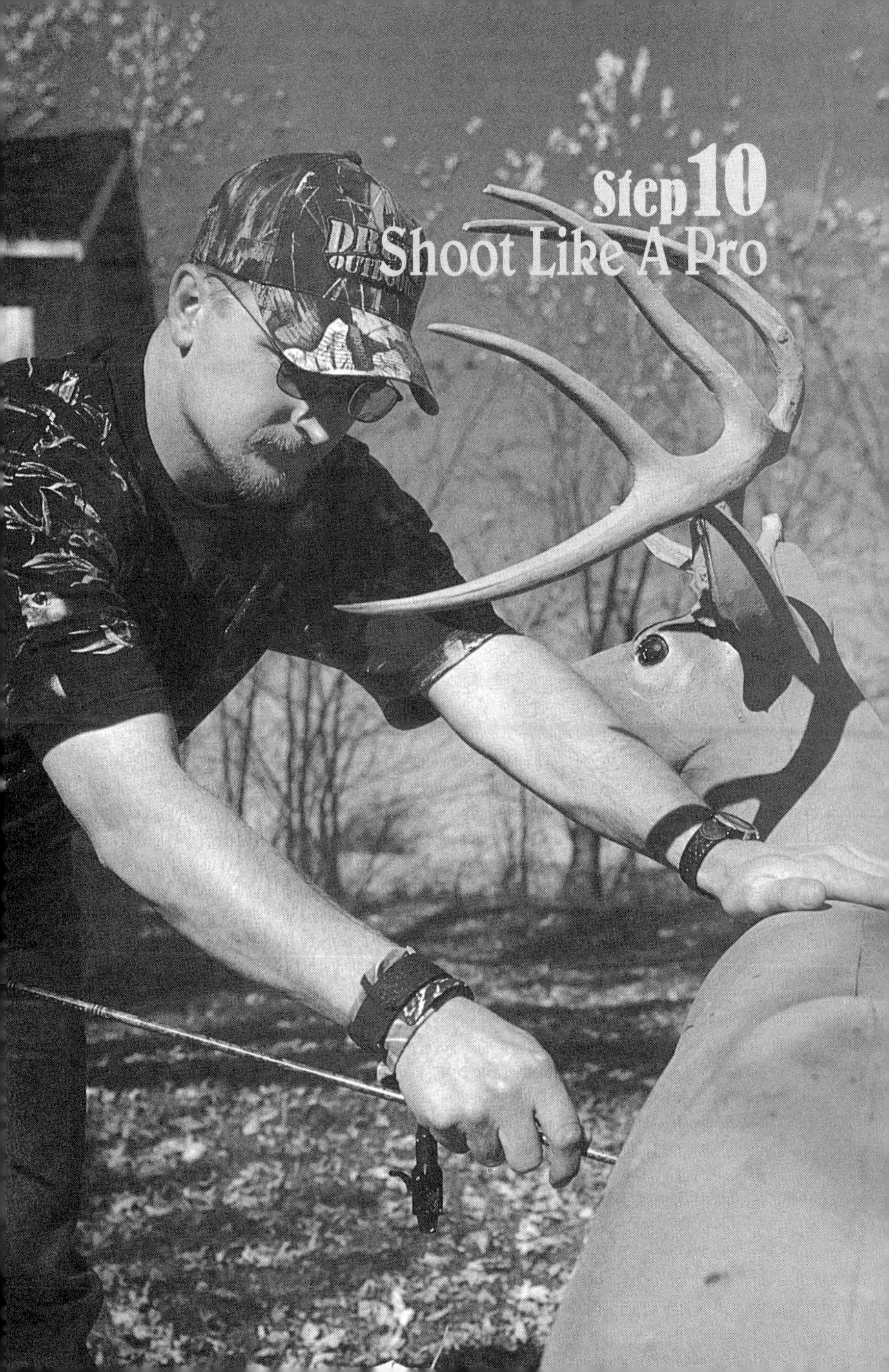

You don't have to be a world-class rifleman to become a deer-hunting machine.

Much of today's high-tech deer hunting gear makes the hunt more enjoyable, but some items can lead to false hopes or expectations. Take compound bows, for example. With the sizzling new one-cam models, many beginning archers, and some seasoned veterans, too, think they're somewhat inferior if they can't place a dozen carbon arrows into a 5-inch pie plate at 40 yards. Likewise, muzzleloading hunters think the new guns and loads should increase their effective range out to 200 yards. Both expectations are highly flawed. For most of us, deer hunting remains a close-encounter proposition. Although some of us are more skilled with a firearm than others, bowhunting remains a 25-yards-or-less deal for 90 percent of all archers.

Knowing your ability and being able to stay within your effective range is the No. 1 key to becoming a highly proficient deer hunter. In fact, some of the most widely recognized names in the hunting industry are guys who take nothing but relatively short shots. I won't name names in this case, because they might be embarrassed to admit they can't "shoot the lights out." No matter. Rest assured that most of the guys you see today holding up great deer are guys who are clutch performers when a deer steps within their shooting range. Sound simple? It should. However, the difference between great and good is huge in the deer woods. The great ones separate themselves from the pack by not only knowing how far to shoot, but precisely when and where to shoot. This chapter provides the information needed for making that transformation.

Simply, a bullet shot into a whitetail's scapula will drop the animal instantly.

The Best Shot for Gun-Hunting

The mature doe tested the wind for a few moments before stepping out from some brambles and onto a logging trail. My heart hammered as I swiveled in the stand and buried the shotgun's stock into my cheek. The doe walked toward the center of the trail and paused when I bleated softly with my mouth. I quickly placed the scope's vertical line on her foreleg and raised the crosshair until it settled on the pie-shaped muscle group about 4 inches below the top of her back.

Boom!

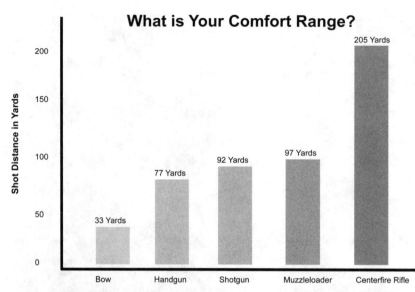

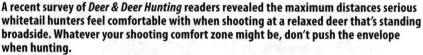

A recent survey of *Deer & Deer Hunting* readers revealed the maximum distances serious whitetail hunters feel comfortable with when shooting at a relaxed deer that's standing broadside. Whatever your shooting comfort zone might be, don't push the envelope when hunting.

All four hoofs left the ground simultaneously, and the doe collapsed in a heap. The deer twitched once or twice, and then all was silent. After crawling down from my stand and tagging the deer, I confirmed my bullet had once again found its mark — square in the scapula (shoulder blade). I said a silent prayer and then began the invigorating task of dragging the deer from the woods and delivering it to a local meat processor for inclusion in my state's venison-donation program. That hunt was one of six successful shotgun hunts I experienced in 2003. All ended with the same result — one-shot kills that dropped the deer dead in its tracks. I could exaggerate and say my shooting skills made those shots possible, but I'd be lying. No, my success hinged merely on a keen understanding of whitetail anatomy. You don't need a magic bullet — or a super-duper slug gun — to mimic such results. In fact, all you need is to learn how to pinpoint — and hit — a target the size of a 5-inch circle, and that's something any gun-hunter should be able to do routinely after a little practice.

One of the most thorough, and perhaps only, scientific studies on shot placement for gun-hunters was conducted by wildlife biologist Charles Ruth and his associates in the South Carolina Department of Natural Resources. In 1999, Ruth unveiled the results of a comprehensive study on bullet, caliber and shot-placement performance for gun-hunters in South Carolina's coastal plain. As reported in the December 1999 issue of *Deer & Deer Hunting*, the researchers examined myriad factors relating to shot performance, hunter behavior and the distance deer traveled after receiving fatal wounds. Although most seasoned gun-hunters know the value of the shoulder-blade shot, the study proved that many hunters have either forgotten its effectiveness or perhaps never realized how deadly it truly is.

This is what happens when you insist on proper shot placement – the deer doesn't go very far.

Simply, a bullet shot into a whitetail's scapula will drop the animal instantly. Death is almost always immediate, with post-shot reactions typically involving involuntary movements of the nervous system.

The South Carolina study involved 493 kills during one hunting season. The mean distance for all shots was 132 yards, and the average distance of killing shots was 127 yards. Of all the kills, 51 percent of the deer dropped when shot. Thirty-four percent of those were killed with shoulder-blade shots; the remaining instant kills were made with neck, spine and head shots. Based on those findings, and assuming spine hits resulted from shoulder-aimed shots going awry, the researchers concluded the shoulder-blade shot is the hands-down most lethal shot for gun-hunters. Deer hit in the scapula traveled an average of just 3 yards, and generally didn't leave the hunter's sight. "The broadside shoulder shot essentially gave results similar to what most hunters expect from a neck shot," Ruth wrote in his report. "Presumably, it works well because it strikes part of the heart and/or lungs, which itself is a mortal blow. However, a shot through the scapula damages the brachial plexus, which is part of the central nervous system, thereby rendering the animal immobile. It knocks the animal out and it never regains consciousness. Also, the shoulder is a large target that offers room for error. A high shot hits the spine; a low shot, the heart; and a rearward shot, the lungs."

Brachial plexus is the scientific name for the network of veins, nerves, tendons and muscles that encompass the shoulder and scapula. To have some fun with your hunting partners, stop reading for a moment and check out the accompanying photo and see if you can identify the center point of the shoulder blade on the doe shown in that photo. If you don't mind temporarily marking up your book, take a pencil (you can erase this afterwards) and have everyone lightly make a small dot on the area that they think is the center of the shoulder blade.

This is a great exercise, because many seasoned hunters get it wrong. In white-tailed deer, the scapula resembles an inverted triangle that is perhaps 5 inches wide at the top, gradually tapering to just over an inch at its connection with the humerus bone. Hitting the shoulder bone squarely with a bullet isn't difficult for a practiced shooter, but it does require intimate knowledge of the scapula's location and how it is repositioned in a deer's skeleton at various leg positions. For example, the scapula/humerus joint points toward a 7-o'clock angle when the foreleg extends forward (example: when a deer steps forward from a broadside position). The joint points to a 4-o'clock angle when the leg completes the step. Granted, this discussion

This 3-D target shows an outline of the exact location of a deer's shoulder blade and leg bone.

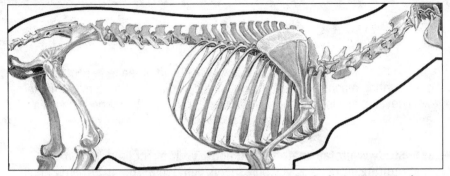

The scapula, or "shoulder blade," is surrounded by a large network of veins, nerves and one major artery. A bullet or slug through this boney plate causes nearly instantaneous death. Bowhunters, however, should avoid aiming for the scapula, because it is difficult to crack with even the sharpest broadhead.

is meant for calculating pinpoint accuracy. A bullet does not have to center punch the scapula to produce an instant kill. In fact, there's some room for error, because a bullet through the forward area of the chest cavity will hit the lungs, liver, diaphragm or heart and put a deer down quickly.

Some folks have told me they prefer to shoot deer in the neck or through the lungs because shoulder-blade shots ruin too much meat. That's nonsense. First, there's little meat on a deer's shoulder to begin with. Shoulder roasts involve nothing more than a flat piece of meat that's not even 2 inches thick. There's much more meat at the base of the neck. I'd rather put a deer down instantly and humanely than worry about losing a couple pounds of less-than-choice venison to bullet damage.

It should also be noted that, when it comes to the shoulder-blade-shot's effectiveness, a deer's size really doesn't matter. I have shot 60-pound doe fawns and 200-pound bucks and have come to one conclusion: Any deer is dead on its hoofs when a bullet squarely hits the scapula.

The shoulder-blade shot is obviously a bowhunter's nightmare. Unlike bullets, which kill by causing major shock and damage to bone and tissue, broadheads kill deer by causing massive hemorrhaging. Some archers shoot enough draw weight to blow arrows through a shoulder blade, but such shots should be avoided at all costs. An arrow through a deer's lungs and/or heart is still the best option for responsible bowhunting. Because many people are now two- and three-season hunters, it's sometimes difficult for avid archers to train themselves to aim for the shoulder blade when they trade their bow for a rifle, shotgun or muzzleloader. Instinct tells them to aim for the deer's lung area, but — as the South Carolina study showed — that shot isn't nearly as deadly as the shoulder-blade shot when gun-hunting

Of course, this discussion requires some preface. A gun-hunter who makes a lung or heart shot on a whitetail ensures himself of the same result: one very dead deer. However, the trailing distance increases over the preferred shoulder-blade shot. According to the South Carolina study, heart-shot deer traveled an average distance of 39 yards after being wounded. Lung-shot deer traveled an average of 50 yards.

HOW TO SHOOT LIKE A PRO

You don't have to be a world-class archer or rifleman to become a deer-hunting machine. In fact, the most successful deer hunters are those who develop proficient shooting skills, and then use their woodsmanship and knowledge of deer anatomy to do the rest.

🦌 **Study whitetail anatomy and know your exact limits when hunting.** If your slug gun only shoots tight groups out to 75 yards, don't shoot beyond that range. Furthermore, knowing where your bullet/arrow will hit is the first step to becoming "automatic." Obtain anatomy charts and study how a deer's internal organs are positioned when the animal stands at various angles. This knowledge will result in clean kills and short blood trails.

🦌 **Strive for placing your centerfire rifle bullet or shotgun slug through the scapula (shoulder blade) of a deer.** A bullet shot into a whitetail's scapula will drop the animal instantly. Death is almost always immediate, with post-shot reactions typically involving involuntary movements of the nervous system.

🦌 **Use soft, rapidly expanding bullets when gun-hunting.** Pinpoint shot placement can make nearly any of today's commercial bullets drop a deer in its tracks every time. Study bullet design well before hunting season and test-fire several different styles. Find one that groups well out of your gun, and stick with it.

🦌 **Use razor-sharp cut-on-contact broadheads when bow-hunting.** Just because broadheads are new doesn't mean they're as sharp as they can be. Always touch up the blades with a sharpener before every hunt. Do not use expandable broadheads unless you shoot 60 pounds of draw weight or more. That much poundage is necessary for expandables to perform as advertised.

🦌 **Insist on taking the quartering-away shot when bowhunting.** Although the broadside shot might appear to present a larger target, it really doesn't. In fact, many hunters argue that the quartering-away shot actually offers a bigger target because a deer's vital area isn't flat like a paper plate. For example, an arrow that enters the paunch and angles forward might miss the near lung, but it will undoubtedly hit the liver and opposite lung as it passes through. Therefore, the quartering-away shot allows for a greater margin of error than any other shot.

Successful bowhunting requires diligent practice, especially during hunting season.

In fact, the worst shot — the gut shot — still resulted in relatively quick kills. Those deer traveled an average of 69 yards. Of course, gut-shot deer — especially those shot through the intestines and not the paunch — can travel much farther.

Instant kills are not only humane, they provide hunters with an option for hunting in today's privatized landscape. Like it or not, our deer-hunting woods aren't what they used to be. Smaller hunting parcels and competition among neighbors is a very real problem for many hunters across North America. Although I haven't experienced this personally, I do know several hunters who aren't allowed to trail wounded deer onto a neighbor's property. That's unfortunate, but it's reality. It should also be motivation for insisting on brachial plexus shots when gun-hunting near property lines.

Although it's important to match a bullet with your firearm, bullet design isn't as critical as you might think — if the bullet, of course, hits its mark. Pinpoint shot placement can make nearly any of today's commercial bullets drop a deer in its tracks every time. Still, bullet design should be studied well before hunting season. Ruth's study concluded that soft, rapidly expanding bullets are best for ensuring

To gain confidence, practice shooting at distances out to 40 yards.

instant kills, or at least short blood trails. I cannot disagree. After shooting dozens of whitetails with shotguns and rifles over the past decade, I've experienced incredible success with factory loads from all the major players. Top shotgun slugs include Winchester's Partition Gold, Federal's Barnes Xpander, Remington's Copper Solid, Lightfield's Hybred EXP, Hornady's H2K and Brennke's Black Magic. Devastating centerfire options include Nosler's Partition, Winchester's Fail-Safe, Remington's Core-Lokt and the Barnes X-Bullet. Put any of these bullets through a deer's scapula, and you'll have an instant addition to your meat pole. Again, accuracy is everything. Matching a cartridge to a gun requires some experimentation, especially for shotgun hunters. For example, the high-velocity Partition Gold is the most accurate slug I've ever shot, but I prefer bolt-action slug guns like the Marlin 512 and Savage 210. Many of my buddies use pumps and auto-loaders, and they have had much more success with lower-velocity rounds.

Before setting slug-shooting goals, remember that consistent long-range accuracy is linked to scoped shotguns with rifled barrels. If you're serious about accuracy, invest in a high quality shotgun scope.

Interestingly, the South Carolina study basically proved that rifle calibers had little impact on killing efficiency. Hunters in the study used five basic calibers: .243, .25, .270, .284 and .30. The mean distance deer traveled after being shot ranged from 14 to 40 yards, and there was no relationship with increasing or decreasing caliber size. Those results shatter several myths, including those surrounding magnum rifles. In other words, a deer shot through the shoulder blade with a .243 will drop just as quickly as one shot with a .300 magnum.

Take your gun-hunting prowess to a new level by learning the exact location of a deer's scapula. Careful observation will teach you how the bladed bone moves in concert with the deer's leg. This knowledge, when teamed with some shooting practice, will help you drop more deer in their tracks. After all, nothing's more satisfying than instant venison.

D&DH's Brad Rucks is one of the best bowhunters the author knows. His success can be directly linked to keen whitetail knowledge and tireless efforts to hone his shooting skills.

The Bowhunting Shot That's Almost Foolproof

The scene would have made most bowhunters ecstatic. With the October sun nearly below the horizon, dozens of whitetails poured out of a distant pine grove and trotted for a lush ryegrass field. Lines of square-nosed does trekked across the field and headed for a secluded corner bordered by white oaks. "That's your corner," the landowner said while handing me a cup of homemade hot apple cider as we stood on his driveway. "There are so many deer out there because we haven't allowed anyone to hunt this land in years. "Shoot as many as you want," he continued. "Just make sure you take clean shots. The neighbor won't let you trail deer on his land."

Talk about pressure. I'm confident in my shooting ability, but restrictions like that make me extra cautious.

I returned to the property the next afternoon with a portable tree stand, four doe tags and high hopes. After hanging the stand high in an oak, I pulled up my bow, quiver and backpack, and settled in for what was sure to be an action-packed hunt.

While nocking an arrow, I couldn't help but think about what the landowner said. Looking down at a well-used deer trail, I decided on the spots where deer had to stand before I could think about shooting. "This arrow doesn't leave my bow-string unless a deer is quartering away," I told myself.

Within 30 minutes, I heard leaves shuffling behind my stand. Leaning into the tree and peering backward, I spied seven deer on the trail. They were beneath my stand in no time. Three of them were mature does. With acorns falling steadily to the forest floor, the deer weren't going anywhere. I decided to shoot the largest doe when given the right opportunity. That took awhile. Although she was standing broadside only 20 yards away, I wanted to be certain my arrow did maximum damage when it hit her. The doe fed for a couple of minutes before lifting her head and turning toward the field.

Thwack!

My arrow hit the doe about 2 inches to the left of where I was aiming, but I wasn't worried. Considering the doe's angle at the moment I shot, I knew she wasn't going far. The doe ran just 45 yards before collapsing. Although I knew the broadside shot would likely have been just as deadly, I was glad I waited for the angling-away shot. The entrance wound was a little far back, but the broadhead sliced the liver, parts of both lungs and the heart.

It seems bowhunters have been taught since birth to wait for the quartering-away shot. It's the best angle, we're told, for causing massive damage to a whitetail's vitals. Hunter education instructors preach the shot's benefits by showing deer anatomy overlays on overhead projectors. The National Bowhunting Education Foundation has even produced a shot-placement video that emphasizes, among other things, the lethality of angling-away shots. Why, then, do some hunters refuse to acknowledge the angling-away shot as the best shot for bowhunting? The answer is rooted in the results of several major bowhunting surveys. *Deer & Deer Hunting* conducted one in 1997 when it asked its readers about their bowhunting habits. More than 2000 hunters responded, providing an error rate of just 3 percent. According to the survey, the average *D&DH* reader would feel comfortable taking a 31-yard shot at a 14-point buck standing broadside. The same hunters said they would only feel comfortable taking a 21-yard shot at a 14-point buck if it was angling away. Here's the amazing part: None of the hunters said they would pass on the 31-yard broadside shot, yet 6.2 percent said they wouldn't shoot if the buck was angling away at 21 yards.

What's even more interesting about the *D&DH* survey is it involved some highly experienced bowhunters. Those responding had an average of 12.7 years of bowhunting experience. In addition, 49 percent had killed a deer while bowhunting the previous year.

These statistics weren't an aberration. The *D&DH* survey was modeled after a study conducted by the Minnesota Department of Natural Resources, which revealed similar tendencies. Jay McAninch, president of the Archery Manufacturers and Merchants Organization, was a wildlife research biologist for the Minnesota DNR in the early 1990s when he supervised a study that asked similar questions. Michael

Osterberg, who presented the findings in his thesis at West Virginia University, conducted the study.

In the study, Minnesota bowhunters were asked to pretend they were in a tree stand and saw a 14-point buck approaching. They were then asked whether they would shoot if the buck was standing at various angles and distances. More than 98 percent of the hunters said they would shoot if the buck was standing broadside at 15 yards. Only 79 percent said they would shoot if the buck was angling away. With the buck standing 40 yards away, 58 percent said they would attempt a broadside shot. Only 22 percent said they would shoot if the buck was angling away at 40 yards.

According to the Osterberg study, a hunter's age can dictate what types of shot angles he prefers. Unfortunately, the study revealed that adults were often more willing to take poor-percentage shots. Of the hunters who said they would attempt a low-percentage shot at a buck standing 15 yards away, 49 percent were age 28 to 42; 30 percent were age 12 to 27; and 21 percent were older than 43. Of the hunters who said they would take a conservative shot — broadside or angling away — at the same distance, 53 percent were age 28 to 42; 30 percent were older than 43; and 17 percent were age 12 to 27. These statistics indicate bowhunters exhibit more confidence with their shooting abilities as they approach middle age, and then revert to conservatism as they mature.

Data from an in-depth bowhunting study at Minnesota's Camp Ripley indicate that hunters are even more reluctant to wait for angling-way shots during actual hunting situations. In her thesis, *Aspects of Wounding of White-tailed Deer by Bow-Hunters*, for West Virginia University, Wendy Krueger found that less than one-third of the successful Camp Ripley bowhunters killed their deer with angling-away shots. According to the 1992-93 study, more than 66 percent of successful hunters waited for broadside shooting opportunities before releasing their arrows. Only 28 percent of successful hunters waited for angling-away shots. The study consisted of four 2-day hunts — two in 1992 and two in 1993. In the four hunts, 7293 hunters killed 693 deer.

McAninch supervised the study. "In approaching this question, we found a bit of discrepant feelings among bowhunters in which shot they thought was better if they were forced to choose," he said. "Clearly, they said they thought the broadside shot presented a bigger target than the quartering shot. In some ways, I agree. If you place a circle around the vitals, the broadside shot presents a bigger target. That seems to shrink when the deer is angling away." Although the broadside shot might appear to present a larger target, it really doesn't. In fact, many hunters argue that the quartering-away shot actually offers a bigger target because a deer's vital area isn't flat like a paper plate. For example, an arrow that enters the paunch and angles forward might miss the near lung, but it will invariably hit the liver and opposite lung as it passes through. Therefore, the quartering-away shot allows for a greater margin of error. Conversely, if a shooter botches a broadside shot and shoots right or left, the arrow will miss the vitals altogether.

Tim Poole, executive director of the NBEF, agrees that the angling-away shot presents the best shot opportunity. "In a way, it's parallel to the issue of not shooting does," Poole said. "In some hunters' minds, the taking of does doesn't make sense. It's not in their scheme of how to manage wildlife. I see the lack of willingness to take the quartering-away shot in a similar fashion. They might rationalize it as less effective. To them, the broadside shot appears to be a better shot. What I don't think they realize is that with the quartering-away shot, they will also shoot the arrow through the diaphragm, liver and possibly a kidney. These are all vital organs, and destroying them results in a clean and quick harvest." Poole was quick to add that although angling-away shots are best for whitetails, they should not be used on bigger animals like elk and moose.

With angling-away shots clearly the better choice, why don't more hunters wait for them? One reason might be because some bowhunters aren't keen on driving an arrow through any part of a deer's paunch because of the mess it might make. Let's hope that's not a wide-held excuse. If it were, bow-hunters would admit to passing on a more effective killing shot in favor of trying to save some field-dressing time. "The whole notion of puncturing the rumen is way overdone," McAninch said. "It's the same thing with the scent glands in (a buck's) legs. People treat them as if they're poison or something. The truth is, even if you slit the rumen, there's almost no way you can ruin the meat. You might lose a backstrap near the abdominal cavity if it gets tainted with stomach contents, but even then you can save almost all of the meat if you just take the time to clean it out. The angling-away shot is so deadly that you shouldn't have to think twice about it."

Granted, an arrow must really go awry, but a hunter can make a mistake on a broadside shot. If the arrow sails 8 or 9 inches right or left, it will hit the abdomen or front shoulder. Even those types of shots can kill deer, but they increase the chances of losing a deer. That possibility is more remote on the angling-away shot, because as the angle becomes more pronounced, a hunter can drive an arrow through a deer's intestines and still hit the liver, a lung and possibly the heart. In short, the angling-away shot almost always kills the animal quickly. Furthermore, the 45-degree angle makes for a much easier passage and entry to the kill zone. "When you take a quartering-away shot, for all practical purposes, you have just improved your chances of killing the deer," McAninch said.

That's not to say McAninch believes hunters should hold out for quartering-away shots at all costs. "In some regards, the quartering-away shot is somewhat tougher to make. This has more to do with experience. The first time you do something — even if it's taking a high-percentage shot — it takes some getting used to." McAninch saw this type of behavior firsthand when he supervised a deer-removal project in a Minnesota suburb. To control a sprawling herd, the community hired FBI-trained sharpshooters. The shooters were instructed to only take head and neck shots at deer as they approached bait stations. Some of the shooters were also hunters, and they struggled with the concept of not aiming for the chest. "These guys could put a bullet on a dime at 500 yards, yet they were apprehensive," McAninch said. "It was a classic case of dealing with the unfamiliar. We all don't like to do things we're unfamiliar with."

McAninch said this phenomenon carries over into the bowhunting debate on shot placement.

HIT WHERE YOU'RE AIMING

❦ Sighting in a rifle or slug gun is probably one of the easiest, yet misunderstood concepts of deer hunting. Most guys have good intentions when they go to the range a few weeks before the season with new cartridges, perhaps a new scope and definitely high expectations. The problem they encounter, however, is they often go without a purpose other than flinging a few rounds at the targets. Precise sighting of a firearm can be accomplished in as little as two shots … if you know what you're doing.

The best advice I've seen on sighting a rifle was published in a press release issued by Pentax Sport Optics about 10 years ago. The method is so simple that I've adopted it as gospel when shooting any new gun/scope combo. The traditional method of sighting a rifle from a solid rest is to aim at the bull's-eye and carefully fire a few shots. The shooter then marks where the bullets hit and adjusts the scope's windage and/or elevation to move the point of impact toward the bull's-eye. The Pentax method is much easier, and usually requires just two shots. The only catch is that it requires two people: a shooter and a spotter.

With the firearm positioned on sandbags or a shooting cradle, the shooter takes aim at the bull's-eye and fires a shot. Immediately after the shot, arrange the rifle back on the bags/cradle and again aim carefully at the bull's-eye. Without moving the rifle, the spotter adjusts the scope's windage/elevation while the shooter peers through the scope. The shooter will actually watch as the crosshairs move. However, instead of moving the crosshairs to the bull's-eye, the shooter makes instructions so they line up with the first bullet hole. This extremely simple routine will result in the rifle shooting exactly where it is aimed. With careful coordination, the second shot should be right on the money. However, depending on the circumstances, it might be necessary to shoot one or two more rounds to fine-tune the scope.

It's common sense that a rifle or shotgun is only as accurate as its condition. In other words, a poorly conditioned gun will very rarely produce consistent groups. This is another often-ignored topic with gun-hunters. The best optics and ammunition won't help much if the bore isn't clean. Rust and sulfur fouling are two of the most common afflictions that affect the accuracy of a deer-hunting gun. To prevent rust, regularly wipe all metal parts with an oily rag. It's equally important to run a solvent-soaked patch through the bore, being extra careful not to scratch the sensitive rifling grooves. Today's array of high-tech solvents and related products makes cleaning extremely easy. Although centerfire guns and shotguns don't require cleaning after every use, it's wise to run at least a few patches through the bore after extended shooting sessions. Even a small amount of fouling can greatly affect shot accuracy.

"I don't know this for a fact, but I think hunters shy away from the angling-away shot because it appears to narrow the shooting window, and the average hunter fights the problem of having a lot of confidence in his shooting ability," he said. "Perhaps they're showing a little bit of conservatism."

McAninch's insights into the behavior of trained sharpshooters probably explain why most hunters feel more comfortable taking broadside shots over angling-away shots at whitetails. In the surveys, most shooters began hunting at younger ages and typically learned how to hunt from their parents. Because most of today's middle-aged deer hunters are first-generation bowhunters, perhaps their inclination for not waiting for angling-away shots was passed down to their children in subtle ways. For example, most archers are guilty of placing their 3-D deer targets in permanent broadside positions. This isn't bad, but it doesn't train shooters to wait and then execute the most devastating shot: the angling-away shot. "You just don't see people practicing angling-away shots," McAninch said. "It's mind-set and habituation. That doesn't mean they don't want to take it. They aren't taking it because they don't think about it. And that goes for guys who know the quartering-away angle is a higher-percentage shot. They've been conditioned to believe the broadside shot is acceptable, so they take it when it comes along."

Shooting schools, hunter education programs and backyard practice sessions have taught us the broadside shot is acceptable for bowhunting. However, this conditioning has perhaps caused many hunters to form a mind block that the broadside shot is the most lethal. It's not. The angling-away shot presents more room for error, and it allows hunters to inflict more damage to a whitetail's vitals, thus increasing the chance for a quicker kill. True, many hunters will argue that "dead is dead" and that they've killed piles of deer quickly and humanely with broadside shots. That's admirable, but it misses the point, which is this: If you have an opportunity to increase your bowhunting success, you should learn more about it. The angling-away shot offers that opportunity.

Step 11
Join The Utilitarian Movement

Ask any seasoned bowhunter and they will probably tell you they were attracted to archery by its beautiful simplicity.

orth America's best deer hunters are those who are more simple, straightforward and practical than high-tech or aesthetic. A truck full of fancy gear and a mind full of science-based tactics are the tools of many modern hunters, but such resources are usually just pacifiers for guys who put relatively few deer on the ground. That approach is fine for some, but it won't ensure an endless backstrap supply, especially in areas where deer hunting hasn't yet evolved to pest management – as it has in many parts of the country. The best ticket to consistent success is to adopt a simple hunting approach and use just what you need – nothing more – to get the job done.

This step on the road to whitetail wisdom includes gear specifics. As is the case with some of the other sections of this book, I've listed some of the products that have worked for me. You can rest assured that these mentions are not made gratuitously; it has always been my motto only to name names when it's relevant and only when I truly believe the product is worthwhile. In that regard, be aware that I have been in the hunting business long enough to know that one man's opinion shouldn't be taken as gospel. What works for me might not work for you. What's more, what's supposedly "the best ever" product today might be eclipsed by something tomorrow.

A quality fiber-optic sight might be the best investment a bowhunter can make.

Simple Bowhunting Gear

The days of noisy, hard-to-shoot compound bows have passed us by. If increased arrow speed and smooth shooting are your goals, visit your local pro shop and shoot a few of today's new bows. Granted, the array of manufacturers and models makes the job of selecting one bow a tall order for some folks. Technology isn't always a good thing, because it sometimes brings trade-offs. The compound bow is a perfect example. Most of us grew up shooting bows with wheels, not cams, and although those bows were fast, they were relatively quiet. Most of today's bows are not. Besides robbing a bow of peak performance, shock and vibration cause premature wear to accessories. Fortunately, today's bow companies have addressed the problem head-on and are now working on more efficient designs.

What's the best bow? That's an impossible question to answer. They're all good. However, all archers – from rookies to seasoned veterans – can't go wrong with a perimeter-weighted one-cam with solid (not split) limbs. In my humble opinion, this configuration is practically foolproof. Most perimeter-weighted single cams feature a coin-sized disc that's placed within the upper end of the cam. When the bow is fired, the weight catapults in the opposite direction of the limbs, counteracting limb movement. The result is drastically decreased recoil and noise and drastically increased accuracy.

Ask any seasoned bowhunter and they will probably tell you they were attracted to archery by its beautiful simplicity. Indeed, the challenge of killing a white-tailed deer with a bow, arrow and broadhead is perhaps the most difficult challenge in hunting. While today's bowhunters still enjoy the challenge, archery is a bit more complicated, especially when it comes to equipment. Hunters must still possess skill and strength to shoot a bow accurately, but they must also know how to use some

Successful bowhunting relies more on a hunter's hunting ability than it does on his gear.

In bowhunting, nothing will put a deer down more quickly than a razor-sharp broadhead through both lungs.

high-tech equipment to achieve the same goal. That high-tech boom is currently going on with archery accessories such as sights, releases and arrow rests.

Rests have come a long way since the days of those little glue-on plastic dealies. There are many choices, including drop-away rests that come with their own video that explains how to install them on your bow. Metal, prong-style rests offer the ultimate in simplicity and utility. The hunter who merely wants to go out and fill tags doesn't need anything more. Among the best prong-style rests are those offered by Tiger Tuff Products. They're easy to adjust and last for years. If you want to step up to something a bit more fancy, the Whisker Biscuit shoot-through rest and Montana Black Gold Trap Door drop-away rest are excellent choices.

Bow sights and other aiming devices fall into another category with seemingly endless possibilities. Today's fiber-optic sights have definitely reached that next level. Combined with the advancements in bows, rests and releases, today's sights are so reliable that most seasoned hunters can shoot accurately out to 30 yards without much problem. My favorite sights are the ones with few moving parts and include tightening devices that ensure pins and components won't wiggle loose after long hours at the practice range. As of this writing, my favorite sights are those made by Trophy Ridge. This company revolutionized the sight industry when it unveiled its lineup of vertical-pin sights. The sights incorporate tightening devices that use wing nuts, not Allen screws. The result is a sight that allows easy adjustments while eliminating the fear of over-tightening an Allen screw and stripping the head. Regardless of your budget, you can find a sight to meet your needs. Remember, not all sights are compatible with all bows. That's why it's important to check out the models from all companies before making a buying decision.

Each year, dozens of hunters ask me what I prefer on my arrows: plastic vanes or natural feathers. Under perfect conditions, I'll pick feathers every time. Although feather fletchings cause more "wind drag" than plastic vanes, feathers are more forgiving off the arrow rest and result in more consistent shots. That's helpful when your shooting form is like mine – far from perfect! That's not to say I don't use vanes. In fact, I've found myself using vanes more often in recent years because they hold up a bit longer and save hassles when I hunt in damp weather. Be wary of short vanes and fletchings. I prefer 4- to 5-inch fletchings. Most competitive target shooters use 3-inch fletchings. Unless you're a tuning freak, don't use fletchings that short. The fletching's job is to stabilize the arrow in flight, so longer is better, especially when shooting cut-on-contact broadheads.

Another common gray area among bowhunters is the dilemma of whether to use straight offset or helical fletchings. Helical fletchings help an arrow rotate. They also help prevent broadheads from planing. Helical is offered in right- and left-hand configurations. Shooting either style is a personal choice, but right-handed shooters typically benefit more from a left-hand fletch, which allows the arrow to spin away from the bow and the arrow rest. When shopping for fletching jigs, be sure to research the various models. If you shoot carbon arrows, you'd be wise to check out the carbon version of the Arizona E-Z Fletch jig. It retails for about $50, but it will save you a lot of time and headaches. Most of the other jigs out there were originally made for aluminum arrows, and, as a result, one can have a hard time adhering fletchings to small-diameter carbon shafts.

Speaking of arrows, I might be old-fashioned, but I'm a tough-sell when it comes to technology. Unfortunately for me, that attitude kept me from improving my archery skills for many years. The arrow debate – carbon or aluminum – is a perfect example. Despite shooting a bow that was capable of blistering speeds, I didn't switch to the lighter carbon arrows until a few years ago. Of course, speed isn't everything. Furthermore, carbon arrows often require upgrading to more expensive rests, quivers and broadheads. When it comes to arrows, remember that just because an arrow is made of carbon or graphite doesn't mean it will fly faster. Speed is directly related to weight. The lighter an arrow, the faster it will fly. However, a light arrow also has a drawback: The lighter the arrow, the less kinetic energy it provides. How fast is fast enough? A bow that shoots 220 to 240 feet per second (ATA) is plenty fast for bowhunting whitetails. In fact, you don't even need that much. In fact, legendary rocker and bowman Ted Nugent swears by the "less is more" mantra. He shoots 500-grain "telephone poles" at just 200 fps from his NugeBow, yet he obtains nearly 100 percent pass-throughs on whitetails. Most important, he makes quick, clean kills. The key? He uses the best cut-on-contact broadheads available and keeps them hair-shaving sharp.

HOW TO JOIN THE UTILITARIAN MOVEMENT

❦ **Keep bowhunting gear simple.** Successful bowhunting relies more on a hunter's hunting ability than it does on his gear. Go with quality, but stick with the basics – nothing more. Leave those stuffed backpacks at home and focus on how to get closer to deer.

❦ **Maintain a sharp edge.** A $700 bow and a $10 carbon arrow are useless if you aren't using a razor-sharp broadhead. If your mission is to kill a deer quickly, opt for a fixed-position broadhead that you can resharpen after every hunt. Sharp broadheads produce tremendous damage to a deer's veins and arteries, causing massive bleeding and quick, humane kills.

❦ **Insist on quality.** The old phrases, "garbage in, garbage out" and "you get what you pay for" certainly applies to hunting. You certainly don't have to have everything in those mail-order catalogs, but don't skimp on what matters most, and that list includes your bow, broadheads and arrows, and your gun, bullets and optics.

❦ **Pack a punch.** A quality cartridge and proven bullet design is to gun-hunting what a sharp broadhead is to bowhunting. Leave the $2-per-box specials to the other guys and step up to a winning combination for your gun.

❦ **Get out there and practice!** Today's high-tech age has brought us many conveniences for deer hunting. None of them are magic. You still need to learn how to shoot and how to perform under pressure to be consistently successful. Don't make the mistake of waiting too long. Bow- and gun-hunting practice should begin in summer and continue throughout the season.

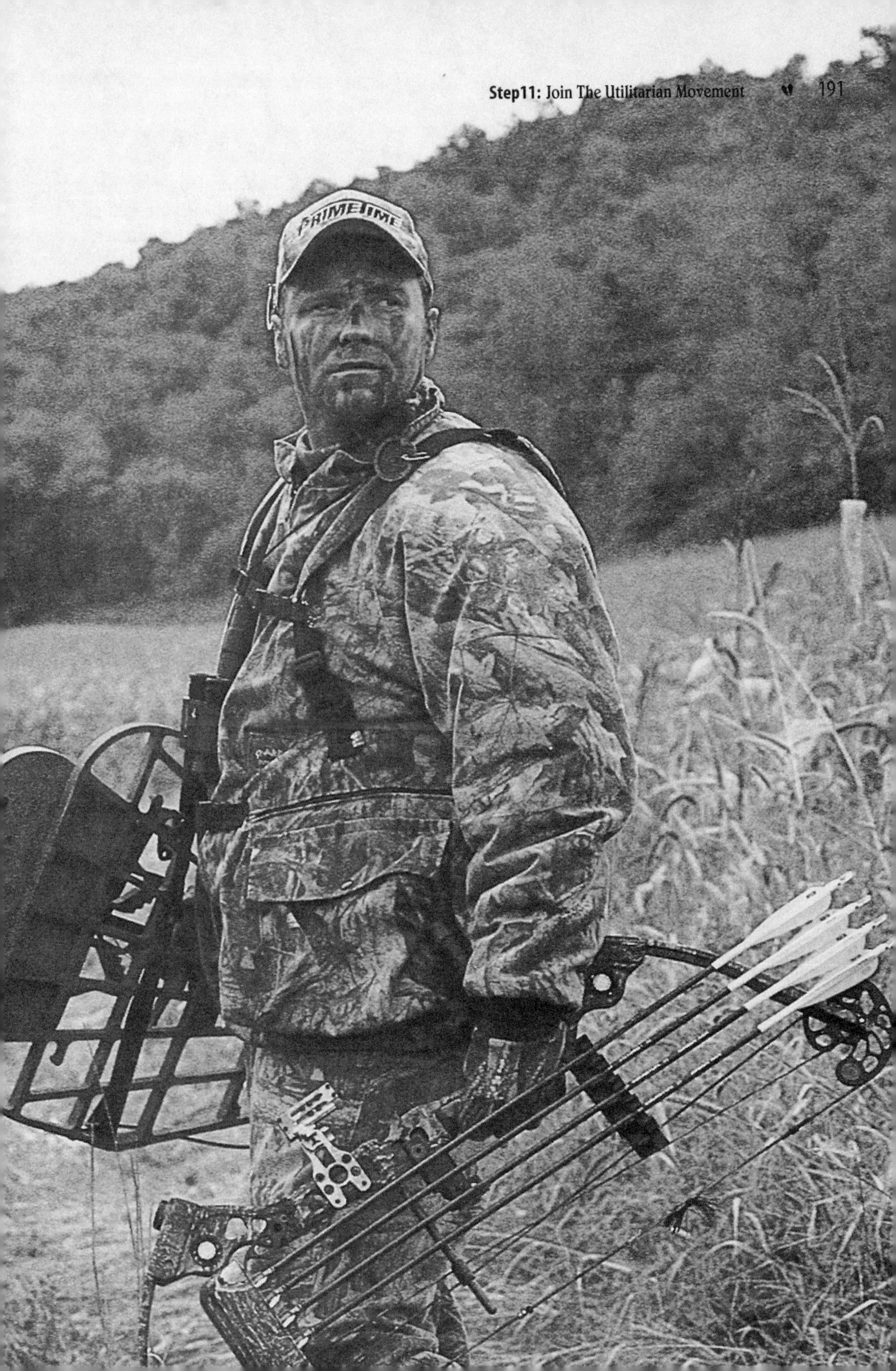

A Few Words on Broadheads

Any well-placed broadhead will quickly and efficiently kill a deer. However, not all broadheads are created equal. Your job in finding the best head for your setup involves finding a broadhead that offers outstanding penetration and cutting ability, indestructible construction and incredible flight characteristics. It might sound like a tall order to fill, but it really isn't in today's market. It requires some hands-on research, however, because every hunter has slightly different needs and tastes.

Technology has certainly pushed broadheads to new levels, but serious hunters cannot overlook traditional designs when shopping for the right head for their setup. Cut-on-contact heads are popular with elk hunters because the blades create

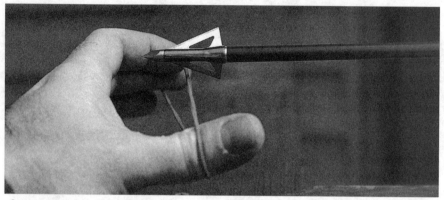

An easy way to test broadhead sharpness is to touch the blades against a taut rubber band. The rubber band should break immediately.

Some expandable broadheads, like the Rocket Aerohead, are true whitetail killers.

massive tissue damage. However, beware that traditional heads can be tricky to shoot, especially if you use a high-speed bow. Wind planing is the No. 1 problem bowhunters encounter when using these broadheads. However, it's worth it to see if your bow can shoot these heads, because they're awfully deadly. The top choices include those heads from Zwickey, Magnus, G-5 and Steelforce.

Replaceable-blade heads are more common and are easier to shoot. Granted, quality broadheads aren't cheap, and it's easy to spend a lot of money trying to determine which one is right for you. The average price for a six-pack of replaceable-blade heads is about $30. You can save money by only using two for practice and spending the extra $15 or so for an extra pack of blades. That way, when it's time to hunt, all you need to do is touch up the tip and replace the blades. Some of the top replaceable-blade heads include the Sullivan Innerloc (my favorite), the standard Muzzy three-blade, Rocky Mountain's Ironhead, Cabela's Lazer Pro Mag, and Satellite's Straight Razor.

It's important to know that most broadheads aren't razor sharp right out of the package. Invest in one of those small, hand-held sharpeners (about $10 to $20 from Cabela's) and sharpen your broadheads before each hunt. Blades become dull by pushing them in and out of a quiver, and they can also lose their edge merely from oxidation. The best test for sharpness is to wind a rubber band in a circle around your thumb and forefinger. You should be able to cut three rubber strands by barely touching them with the edge of the broadhead's blades. Another test is to shave hair off the back of your arm. By all means, be careful when doing these tests!

Mechanical broadheads became the rage in the archery industry in the mid-1990s when two things – 3-D archery and high-speed bows – became more popular. Hunters realized they could shoot farther and more accurately with broadheads that flew more like field points. The logic was sound, but many hunters, myself included, stubbornly stuck with their tried-and-true heavy arrow/broadhead combinations. With today's craze of being bigger, better and faster, it's difficult not to adapt to the new wave of bowhunting. In other words, if your bow is a Cadillac, you had better feed it premium.

It's easy to zing broadheads through stationary objects – cinder blocks, steel cans, cardboard – under controlled circumstances and proclaim one better than another. Although insights from such tests are valuable, they don't come close to simulating what happens when blade meets living bone. With that in mind, I have spent the past six archery seasons shooting as many different types and brands of broadheads as possible. In fact, I spent the 1999 and 2000 seasons shooting nearly nothing but expandables. Liberal antlerless seasons allowed me to practically buy as many doe tags as I wanted, and I responded by shooting 16 deer with 13 different expandables. Although all of the heads achieved desired results – they killed deer – the experiment eventually prompted me to revert back to my old ways and shoot replaceable-blade broadheads. It was merely a personal decision based on the fact that I prefer to hone my broadheads after every hunt, and this luxury is not practical when using expandables. In case you're wondering, the top performers in my field tests were the heads manufactured by Mar-Den, Rocket Aeroeheads, Satellite and Rocky Mountain Archery.

No More Pumpkin Lobbers

Some hunters still rely on smoothbore shotguns and iron beads for slug-hunting. They don't know what they are missing. With today's rifled slug guns and high-tech slugs, hunters can greatly improve their accuracy and effective range.

Winchester Ammunition took shooting to a new level when it introduced the Winchester Supreme Partition Gold slug in 2000. Never before had a sabot shot so accurately and provided so much knockdown power for long-range shots at whitetails. I've shot this slug almost exclusively ever since, and it has produced dozens of impressive one-shot kills. This discussion, however, requires some prefacing. First, the Partition Gold gains much of its accuracy from the fact that it's a smaller-diameter slug. Therefore, it produces somewhat smaller entry and exit wounds – and less-impressive blood trails on deer shot through the chest cavity. Second, the slug does not shoot well out of all shotguns. In fact, many slug-shooters I know have a hard time getting it to print tack-driving groups when shooting the slug from certain pump-action and semi-automatic shotguns. In my tests, the slug is an absolute prizewinner when shot out of a bolt-action slug gun like those made by Marlin and Savage. Out of those guns, this slug can easily print tight groups at 150 yards.

My best experience with the Partition Gold came on opening morning of Wisconsin's 2000 gun season. My wife and I were sitting in a natural ground blind that overlooked a freshly cut alfalfa field. Deer had been feeding in the field both mornings and evenings – a great spot to "make some venison." Imagine our surprise when, shortly after daybreak, the skies clouded over and it started to snow!

Undaunted, we pulled on our knit hats and hunkered in for a long sit. After an uneventful hour, we were jolted to high-alert status by some breaking branches and the telltale "thump-thump" of deer hoofs coming from a nearby creek bottom.

Although modern pumps and semi-autos make for decent slug guns, nothing beats a scoped bolt-action with a rifled barrel.

Within moments, Tracy noticed a deer moving up from the creek bottom toward the field edge. "He's way down there," she whispered while crooning her neck and motioning with her head. I slowly peered out from one of the blind's downed oak limbs. "Oh, geesh, he's going to cut across the field right there," I said disappointedly. "That's too far for your gun."

"He looks like a good one," she replied, as the buck stood in some high grass, swirling his nose into the air to test the wind. "If you can take him, take 'em." "You sure?" I replied, somewhat hesitant, because I had wanted Tracy to take the first deer. "Yes!" she hissed. "We might not get another chance at a buck like that!"

I slowly reached for my rangefinder and lasered the buck: 167 yards. Weeks of practicing shots at 150 yards gave me the utmost confidence for this shot. I must add, however, that previous conversations with my good friend Dave Henderson – the nation's top slug-gun writer – helped me realize the true capabilities of my gun and cartridge. Henderson had previously told me to practice at 150 yards, because the ballistics of the Partition Gold would allow me to sight-in the gun dead-on at 150 yards and still make shots out to 180 yards. He also told me that I could make shots all the way out to 190 yards if I held 2 inches high and allowed for 6 inches of drift. I wasn't about to take a shot that far. Still, this buck was within the range I had practiced, so I knew I could make the shot. All I had to do now was find a solid rest. Slowly inching forward, I pressed the shotgun flat atop a thigh-sized oak limb and buried the stock into my cheek and shoulder. The rest was so solid that I felt like I was at the shooting range. I had about 15 seconds to control my breathing before the buck stepped into the field. As the scope's crosshairs settled high on his shoulder blade, I exhaled and squeezed the trigger simultaneously. BOOM! Although the shot nearly knocked me on my butt, I was still peering through the scope when I saw the puff of smoke exit the barrel. The buck mule-kicked and ran 75 yards before collapsing. The shot missed its mark by about 2 inches, but it still center-punched both lungs and led to one extremely satisfying hunt.

I must admit that Tracy and I were both somewhat surprised we got that deer. Although I'm a confident hunter, I know full well that my success on that day would never have happened had I not been using such top-end gear. If anything, it proves that anyone with average shooting skills can be successful if they take the time to match the right bullets with the right gun and spend just a modest amount time practicing before the season.

Remember, the best slug for my shotgun might not be the best for yours. It's critical that you testfire several different slugs, because each gun is different. Also note that ballistics vary with each load. The Hornady H2K is the fastest slug available. It's the first commercially made shotgun slug to surpass the 2000-fps threshold. However, the Federal Barnes X-Pander (1800 fps) and the Winchester Partition Gold (1840 fps) are equally impressive. Although the Partition Gold shoots best out of my gun, the Federal load has a more impressive bullet. In fact, the X-Pander just might be the best bullet ever designed for whitetails. The one-piece design features six perforated petals that peel backward upon impact, creating one nasty-looking mushroom that creates awesome wound channels. Another top choice is the Remington BuckHammer.

BEING A UTILITARIAN CAN SAVE YOU MONEY

❧ A wise man once said, "Everything in life comes back to circle." I'm not positive, but he must have been a bowhunter. After a decade of experimenting with various broadheads, I decided in 2004 to switch back to the chisel-tipped, replaceable-blade broadheads – like the ones I first used when I first took up bowhunting.

As any bowhunter knows, broadheads and arrows don't come cheaply. In fact, a guy practically needs to set up a savings account just to pay for all the accessories he goes through in any given season. I'm no different. With our toddler plowing through the Pampers and seemingly endless Sesame Street videos, I'd become a better utilitarian when it came to my bowhunting addiction. I wasn't giving up my Robin Hood ways of shooting surplus deer and donating them to charity; instead, I would make better use of my broadheads and arrows.

I started by switching to a low-price quality shaft – Stalker Extreme carbons sold by Cabela's. I watched the sales catalogs and picked up a dozen fletched arrows for $39, plus tax. I had used these arrows in the past and honestly couldn't see a difference in flight characteristics beyond 30 yards. As for broadheads, I wanted the best-made replaceable-blade heads I could find, because that would allow me to re-use heads throughout the season. I settled on a six-pack of Sullivan Innerlocs, which I had found to be unbelievably tough during some extensive broadhead testing in the late 1990s. These heads weren't cheap ($30 for six), but I figured they'd withstand my constant abuse. I also ordered a pack of 18 replacement blades ($15).

The plan paid off big time. Halfway through the season, I had bagged four deer with the same arrow and broadhead. Granted, I had to change the broadhead's blades twice, but the ferrule and tip were not worse for the wear. Unfortunately, the arrow was broken on the fourth deer. Still, this is a good example of how to save money without sacrificing quality. That arrow/broadhead combo cost me (including the extra blades) $13.25, or just $3.31 per deer. Not a bad investment for a pile of prime venison!

Centerfire Concerns

Bryce Towsley is a great friend of mine who happens to be one of the nation's top gun writers. I've often razzed him about the fact that he's been a gun geek for almost as long as I've been alive, but he seems OK with that. The one thing Towsley has on every other gun writer, however, is the fact that he's more interested in killing deer than fingering a calculator to determine ballistics data. When I was a pup in this industry, Towsley unknowingly took me under his wing and taught me everything I needed – or really cared – to know about centerfire rifles and cartridges for whitetail hunting. His best advice was a five-point agenda related to ammunition, but it applies to rifle selection. When I asked him to list the best ammo choices for deer hunting, he prefaced the whole discussion by asking, then answering a list of questions.

1. What do want? Are you a long-range shooter? If so, you need a bullet that shoots flat trajectories and causes positive, low-velocity expansion.

2. Do you prowl thick brush? If so, a flat-shooting, low-velocity expansion bullet isn't for you.

3. What type of deer do you hunt? You'll need different bullets if you hunt blocky, winter-hardened Northern bucks one week and smallish Texas bucks the next.

4. What kind of rifle do you shoot? A short-action 7mm-08 Remington calls for different loads than the new breed of powerhouses like the .300 Remington Ultra Mag. Although the same bullet could kill deer in all of the above scenarios, that doesn't mean they will perform equally.

The Winchester Partition Gold is one of the most accurate shotgun slugs on the market.

5. What kind of performance do you want? A popular theory – one that Towsley doesn't subscribe to – states a bullet should stay in a deer's body to "dump all of its energy." "Whitetails are small critters," he said. "To stay in a deer, a bullet has to be soft, allowing it to come apart on impact. True, such a bullet, when shot through a modern rifle, can produce spectacular results. However, that's not always the case."

In short, Towsley says a controlled-expansion bullet shot through a modern rifle will ensure ultimate penetration and a clean kill. The bullet results are not as spectacular as, say, those from a soft bullet, and hunters must often track deer after the shot. However, he added that dependable expansion and deep penetration will assure hunters that they will follow the blood trail to a dead deer every time.

Be Smart, But Don't Be Cheap

It's one thing to be a "poor but practical" hunter, and it's another to be a cheapskate. The biggest mistake I see hunters make year after year is they rush out and buy the

Bullets that provide dependable expansion and deep penetration will assure hunters that they will follow the blood trail to a dead deer every time.

Confidence in your equipment is ultimately the No. 1 key to being consistently successful in the whitetail woods.

best gun and ammo and then totally skimp on optics. It absolutely doesn't make sense, and, in fact, it's downright foolish. People hate to hear it, but the best advice when shopping for a scope is to expect to pay as much, if not more, for your rifle or shotgun scope than what you paid for the gun itself.

When it comes to scopes, quality comes with a high price tag mainly because good glass requires long curing times. The best scope glass takes months to cure. Also adding to the cost are the new high-tech coating processes. Although most manufacturers fully coat all glass surfaces, some do not. Before buying a scope, make sure all air-to-air glass surfaces of each lens are coated. This greatly enhances the scope's ability to gather light and increases performance in low-light conditions. Technology has also brought us the new lens coatings that prevent a scope from fogging up or retaining moisture during cold, wet and/or humid weather.

The scope's reticle (crosshair) type is also important. Match it to how, when and where you hunt. A thin reticle is ideal for hunting midday. There are seemingly endless options, including flash-dot reticles that project a light beam to the scope's aiming point and illuminated reticles that contrast sharply with the target.

Scopes come in all shapes, sizes and price ranges. It's important to remember that no single factor will make or break the way a scope works. What you want is a combination of good glass, solid construction, proper reticle and multi-lens coatings.

Step **12**
Stay On Track

Deer blood has high levels of Vitamins K1 and K2, which is found in the foods they eat. These vitamins feature an anti-hemorrhagic agent that speeds the blood-clotting process.

The most frustrating blood trail is one that's out of your control. I experienced such a trail a few years ago when bowhunting the land of a highly seasoned bowhunter. On the first afternoon of my hunt, I arrowed a mature doe. Although I intended to wait an hour before taking up the trail, the skies unexpectedly turned dark, and it started raining. I immediately climbed from my stand and started trailing the deer. I trailed the doe for about 200 yards when the landowner showed up. After a half-hearted effort in helping me trail the deer, he called off the mission. "To hell with it," he said. "We're going back to camp. After all, it's just a doe. Besides, we'll spook all of the big bucks out of here if we mess around in here for very long." That happened years ago, but I still get a sick feeling in my stomach when I think about it. Needless to say, that was the first and last time I hunted with that guy.

If you hunt for long, you're bound to shoot a deer you won't recover. It's frustrating, but it happens. However, there are certain things you can do to prevent it. First and foremost, pick your hunting partners carefully. Second, don't go hunting when you're strapped for time. If you're planning to hunt for four hours, give yourself 10. You never know how long it will take you to recover your deer and get it out of the woods. In fact, the key to staying on track has more to do with your blood-trailing approach than it does to your experience or skill. Granted, successful blood trailing requires basic knowledge of a deer's anatomy, but consistent success hinges more on extreme patience and persistence.

Win the Mental Game

To increase your recovery success rate, take mental notes immediately after every shot. Memorize three things: where the deer was standing when it was shot; how it reacted to the shot; and the exact place where it was last seen. Did the deer bound away? Was its tail up or down? Did it fall down at any point during its escape? These might sound like minor details, but they can be very helpful after the fact when trying to locate and piece together the blood trail. It's most important to note the exact spot where the deer was last seen.

This tactic helped me find a hog-bodied buck I shot in Wisconsin recently. My stand was at the edge of an oak ridge, overlooking a meadow and a small food plot. The buck stepped into shooting range just minutes before shooting time expired. My shot felt and looked good, but everything happened so fast that I didn't see the arrow hit him. He bucked, whirled and sprinted for a brush-choked fence line. I lost sight of him when he passed a large red oak that stands in the middle of the meadow. Although that visual would normally have been an adequate marker, I pulled out my binoculars and focused on a clump of grass near the tree that seemed to better indicate the last spot where I had seen the buck. That minor detail wound up paying major dividends.

Just to be safe, I quietly descended my stand and retreated through the woods to a spot where my wife had been hunting. We decided to walk back to the landowner's house and wait for an hour before taking up the blood trail. We no sooner got to the house than it started pouring rain. The landowner's son, Shane, asked me to recall the buck's escape route. "Well," I said. "I don't know how far he ran, but I do know that he ran past an old tire by that big oak tree in the meadow."

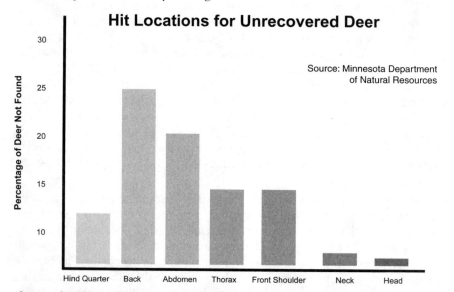

Hit Locations for Unrecovered Deer

Source: Minnesota Department of Natural Resources

Percentage of Deer Not Found (y-axis: 10, 15, 20, 25, 30)

Hind Quarter · Back · Abdomen · Thorax · Front Shoulder · Neck · Head

A comprehensive bowhunting study in Minnesota showed that archers wound relatively few deer that are not recovered. As indicated here, of the wounded deer that are not recovered, wounds are often superficial.

"I know that spot like the back of my hand," Shane said. "There's a heavy trail that leads right past that tire. It loops around that small waterhole." Shane was right, and, after deciding to wait until daybreak to resume the trail, we found the blood trail – and the dead buck – about 75 yards from that old tire. This is just one of dozens of blood trails I've been on over the years where a seemingly inconsequential detail collected immediately after the shot helped locate a dead deer.

Tips for Locating Your Deer

Much has been written about tracking and trailing white-tailed deer over the years, but a few points are often overlooked. Successful trailing doesn't require complicated strategies, but it does require that hunters pay close attention to simple details. Incorporate the following six rules into your game plan, and you'll drastically improve your trailing success rate.

1. Use a compass. A simple compass reading just after the shot can point you in a straight line toward your dead deer. A lot of guys merely use the sun's position in the sky for direction. That can provide a ballpark estimate, but it's not as reliable as a compass reading.

2. Don't assume. Trying to think like a deer is a good strategy for finding stand sites, but it's highly inaccurate when following a blood trail. Some hunters claim wounded deer won't climb hills, cross open fields or wade streams. Nonsense. Deer do not possess rational thought. Rule out nothing, and literally leave no stone unturned when searching for blood.

Closely study the arrow from all pass-through hits. It can tell you a lot about how badly a deer is wounded.

3. Don't obsess. Never give up on a blood trail just because it's sparse. That's a huge mistake. Many hunters assume a deer isn't fatally wounded when they've trailed it a few hundred yards and only found sporadic droplets. Deer have thick layers of tallow along their backstraps, as well as around their organs. Fat can easily plug a wound, making the resulting blood trail seem like it came from a superficial wound. While bowhunting a few years ago, I shot a mature buck high through one lung and low through the other. The deer wheeled and sprinted about 200 yards into a thick clearcut. He died within a minute, but it took us three hours to unravel his blood trail. The arrow was coated with tallow, and the blood trail was nothing more than a few drops every 10 yards or so. The exit wound, near his armpit, was completely plugged with fat.

Legendary outdoor writer Jim Casada told me of a similar blood trail he experienced while gun-hunting at Alabama's White Oak Hunting Plantation. Casada said the shot felt good, but there was little visual evidence that he actually hit the deer, even though his hunt was caught on film. After searching for 30 minutes, Casada and expert guide Bo Pitman found some hair. "Still, there was no blood at the site of the shot, and for 50 yards nothing," Casada said. "Then, Bo found single drops at six or eight places, none of them closer than 10 yards to the previous one. A couple of broken sticks and one stagger spot helped, and finally, 150 yards later, he found where the deer had stood and bled maybe 15 drops. Ten yards later, almost all of this was in a dense thicket, he found the deer. My shot had been near perfect, but something, probably some bone or cartilage, had stopped up the holes."

4. Put your pride aside. Under the "it's not sexist if it's true" department: Overall, women are better than men at seeing blood on the ground. If you don't believe me, take your wife, daughter or girlfriend on your next blood trail and test this hypothesis for yourself. I was absolutely amazed when I took my wife on her first blood-trailing excursion. Tracy's keen eyes helped me find a deer I might have very easily given up on. Since then, she has unraveled many puzzling trails. Her ability to find pin-sized blood droplets in pine needles is flat-out amazing.

In fact, a recently completed Arizona State University study concludes that women possess a gene that allows them to see varying shades of red much better than men. According to the researchers, the gene is linked to the X chromosome. Because women have two X chromosomes (men have just one), their ability to see into the red/orange spectrum is believed to be twice as good as men. According to a report in the *American Journal of Human Genetics*, Dr. Brian Verrelli and Dr. Sarah Tishkoff made the conclusions after studying DNA samples from nearly 250 men from various countries. The report also noted that while 8 percent of all men are colorblind, few women suffer from the malady because their twin X chromosomes all but prevent it.

5. Take some measurements. Depending on region and age, white-tailed deer stand about 36 inches high at the shoulder. Some Southern deer are a few inches shorter, while some Northern deer are a tad taller. This information helps the hunter gauge a wound's location when he's following a blood trail through high vegetation. If you're finding consistent blood smears 30 inches high or higher on saplings and

A deer has about 1 ounce of blood for every pound of total body weight. Furthermore, a deer must lose one-third of its blood supply before death will occur.

such, chances are the arrow or bullet entered high through the lungs or possibly missed them altogether. Contrary to popular belief, there is no such thing as an empty space between the spine and the lungs. According to respected deer researcher Jay McAninch, formerly of the Minnesota Department of Natural Resources, a deer's chest cavity is pressurized, and any disruption of these sensitive membranes will cause death in a whitetail, but it might take longer than usual. However, that's the topic of another section. In short, if the blood trail indicates a high hit, be prepared for the possibility of a longer tracking effort.

6. Size 'em up. When it comes to whitetails, the old saying, "the bigger they are, the harder they fall" certainly rings true. All deer have amazing survival instincts, but mature bucks – those 3-1/2 years old and older – seemingly can cover a lot of ground even after a hunter makes a picture-perfect shot. This surely has to do with the larger size of an adult deer, which, in turn, is related to its blood capacity. According to famed naturalist Leonard Lee Rue III, a deer has about 1 ounce of

Never give up until you've exhausted every option, even if you temporarily lose the blood trail.

blood for every pound of total body weight. He also states that a deer must lose one-third of its blood supply before it dies. This information provides some valuable insights when one compares deer on both ends of the spectrum.

In 2003, I killed several deer with double-lung shots while bowhunting. One was a mature buck that weighed more than 270 pounds on the hoof. Even though the razor-sharp broadhead center-punched the back lobes of the buck's lungs, the deer ran about 200 yards and lived approximately 90 seconds after the shot. Later in the season, I made an almost identical shot on a 72-pound doe fawn. That deer only ran 20 yards before collapsing dead in its tracks. Why such a drastic difference? Well, the buck had to lose more than 5 pints of blood to die, while the doe fawn had to lose just 1-1/2 pints.

Whitetails have extraordinary healing powers, and studies indicate this phenomenon comes from the green, leafy vegetation they eat throughout spring and summer. For unknown reasons, deer blood can store high levels of Vitamins K1 and K2. These vitamins feature an anti-hemorrhagic agent that speeds the blood-clotting process. Even more amazing, deer acquire these levels by the time they're just 4 months old. It has also been proven that a deer's brain can release high levels of B-endorphins to deal with trauma. It is believed these high endorphin levels control pain and, therefore, allow deer to flee farther distances after suffering fatal wounds.

7. See the light. A small penlight or cheap handheld flashlight won't suffice on nighttime trails. Bring lights that will get the job done. The best lights I've used are an old Coleman lantern and the NiteLite headlamp used commonly by coon hunters. Two people need at least one lantern, two headlights and two spare midsized handheld flashlights for backups. Carry plenty of extra batteries. Other equipment: a roll of blaze-orange tape, a GPS unit, bottled water, granola bars, nuts or raisins for energy, and, most importantly, biodegradable toilet paper for marking blood sign. A tissue trail not only points you in the right direction, it can easily help you decipher the trail if you must call off the effort and return in daylight.

Deer do not possess rational thought. Rule out nothing, and literally leave no stone unturned when searching for blood.

HOW TO STAY ON TRACK

❦ **Get serious.** Treat every wounded deer with the respect it deserves. Blood trailing is not the time for fooling around and lighting the woods up with laughter and barroom conversations. Talk should be limited to soft whispers and reserved for sharing observations and strategies.

❦ **Appoint a team leader.** Whatever he says goes – no ifs, ands or buts. The lead trailer should be the one with the most experience and the most patience. On two-person teams, the leader picks his position, which is usually "tracker."

❦ **Take control of the situation.** When it comes to blood trailing, three's a crowd. Only allow a third person to enter the picture when a trail requires a roamer. This tracker carefully circles ahead of a lost trail in hopes of relocating blood sign. This person must be willing to take detailed instructions from the team leader, because they can easily disturb previously unseen blood, scuff marks, overturned leaves, etc.

❦ **Never assume.** And, contrary to my previous advice on scouting for hunting spots, avoid thinking like a deer when following a blood trail. Wounded whitetails can exhibit predictable behavior, but they can also do bizarre things you would never imagine.

❦ **Keep coyotes in mind.** If the property you hunt holds a sizable coyote population, consider trailing every deer (except gut-shots) immediately. The risk of pushing a mortally wounded deer is often outweighed by the risk of losing it to scavengers.

Lung Shots

Bowhunters should always strive for the double-lung hit. This shot provides consistently quick kills, especially when the arrow is shot at a deer that is quartering away from the hunter. Lung hits are typically characterized by pink, frothy blood that may or may not exhibit bubbles (the presence of oxygen in the blood). Be warned, however, that blood trails from lung hits come in myriad forms. Lung-hit deer do not always leave blood at the hit sight, and arrows that pass through a deer's lungs are not always covered with blood. The deer still die quickly, but the trails can sometimes be downright puzzling.

The best example of a double-lung hit exhibiting sparse sign came when I shot a buck at the close of the 1990s. The buck was mere feet from my stand when I sent an arrow through his chest cavity. The arrow went through him so quickly that I did not see exactly where it hit him. The buck bolted for about 50 yards, stopped and did an about-face before charging off into a thick pine grove. I did not hear him go down, so I sat patiently and waited for darkness. I was certain of a good hit, so you can imagine my surprise when I crawled down and found my arrow covered with nothing but a thin smear of tallow. The only blood sign was a slight hint of red on my otherwise all-white feather fletchings. It took my wife and I nearly 30 minutes to

It might sound cliché, but good, old-fashioned persistence is the key to finding every deer you shoot.

All deer have amazing survival instincts, but mature bucks – those 3.5 years old and older – seemingly can cover a lot of ground even after a hunter makes a picture-perfect shot.

find the first spot of blood on the ground, which, by the way, was located 75 yards from the hit sight. From there we followed a spotty trail – a drop here and there – until we found the buck. He had died on the run just 125 yards from the stand. The arrow had hit him a tad high but angled down and nearly center-punched the left lung. It exited low through the opposite lung, just below the right armpit area. The tallow came from the entry wound area and likely caused the wounds to clog.

I've also been on blood trails where either I or another hunter has shot an arrow nearly parallel through a deer's lungs where blood was not found anywhere near the hit site. This happens because lung-shot deer often suffocate as their lungs fill up with blood from the wounds. Much of the blood that does make it to the ground is sprayed from the deer's mouth. This makes for blood trails that appear as misty sprays or the drop-here-drop-there variety. Another point worth mentioning is that big deer can run a long distance with a single-lung wound. They will die, but it can make for a long trail. That's why it's best to wait at least 30 minutes to an hour before trailing any mortally wounded deer. I'll address the topic of waiting more later, but, all things being equal, it's often the best approach for trailing mortally wounded whitetails.

Liver Shots

Most veteran hunters can identify the liver-shot deer, but many incorrectly assess this situation. A liver hit is characterized by dark-red blood, and typically lots of it, at the hit site. The bowhunter might find his arrow coated with this maroonish blood, and the arrow will usually also have paunch or intestinal material on it, resulting in a foul odor. The liver-shot deer often reacts violently and crashes away at the shot, but it often slows to a walk after a short distance. The presence of lots of blood makes most hunters believe this shot will put the deer down quickly. Such is not always the case. In fact, liver-shot deer often live long enough that they don't die until after they've bedded. For this reason, it's wise to let a suspected liver-shot deer go for 2 to 3 hours before trailing it.

Although some blood-trailing rules call for hunters to wait before trailing wounded deer, all bets are off when you're hunting areas thick with coyotes. This Nebraska buck was found within just a few hours after suffering a fatal wound from a muzzleloader.

Liver-shot deer commonly leave trails that bleed profusely immediately after the shot, then slow to a trickle. Never quit on a trail just because blood slows. Wherever there's blood, there's hope for recovery. Over the years, I've found several deer that other hunters gave up on because the deer "wasn't bleeding enough." Even the most fatal of wounds can easily become clogged with fat, muscle and even stomach contents.

Rumen and Intestinal Wounds

A bullet or arrow anywhere through a deer's abdomen is usually referred to as a gut shot. What some hunters don't realize is that not all gut shots are the same. The rumen (stomach) shot is probably most common because it is located directly behind the liver. The intestines are even farther back – located in the cavity just ahead of the hips.

A deer's reaction to a bullet or arrow through the rumen is characterized by the animal humping up and walking or trotting slowly from the scene. Bowhunters often find stomach contents (partially digested food) on their arrows, and notice a foul odor. In snow country, blood trails often appear with brownish/greenish streaks in the snow. Hunters should wait at least 4 hours before trailing a rumen-shot deer. In fact, it's better to wait 6 to 8 hours, especially when weather conditions permit it. These deer typically travel a short distance and bed. If left undisturbed, they will die shortly thereafter. All rumen-shot deer will die, but the distance traveled greatly increases when deer are pushed.

A bullet or arrow through the large or small intestines is a true gut shot. These deer will also die in their beds if undisturbed, but hunters should wait at least 10 hours – no matter the circumstance – before trailing them. Gut-shot deer will run great distances if pursued immediately.

I know many seasoned hunters, including outdoor writers John Trout of Indiana and Richard Smith of Michigan, who find nearly every gut-shot deer they encounter. It's not that they're lousy shooters – in fact, they are usually called in to track deer for other hunters. What makes such trackers so successful? Patience ... and a lot of it.

"You have to be able to put aside all your preconceived notions about trailing and deer behavior," Trout once told me. "And you have to dedicate yourself to staying on that track no matter how long it takes to unravel it." His words spoke volumes, and I've lived by them ever since. All too often I see hunters who merely give up because "the deer couldn't have been hit that hard," or "he should have died by now." Those are lame excuses from irresponsible hunters. Another poor excuse is the often-exaggerated distances that hunters claim to have trailed their deer before giving up. Most guys talk in "miles," when in reality they probably trailed the deer for a few hundred yards. Time spent looking for blood sign is usually the culprit for such claims. Unraveling small drops of dried blood on oak leaves or pine needles can literally take hours. Don't fret about the dinner you're missing or about getting to work on time. Call your loved ones and tell them you have something important to finish up on, or call in sick to work. After all, you shouldn't have gone hunting in the first place if you didn't expect to shoot a deer. You owe it to the animal to make every effort to recover it, even if that means coming back the next day or possibly the day after that.

NEVER ASSUME ... AND NEVER GIVE UP

❦ Few things in hunting are more frustrating than gut-shooting a deer. It might sound cliché, but good, old-fashioned persistence is the only way to find every deer you shoot. The best example I've seen of this attitude was displayed many years ago during a wilderness hunt when my hunting partners unraveled a truly bizarre blood trail.

The episode began at 7:30 a.m. when my brother Tony was walking a logging trail. A buck appeared on the trail before him, and he quickly shouldered his rifle and shot. The buck mule-kicked and sprinted for a dense stand of birch and aspen. Tony thought the shot hit the buck a little far back, but he was certain it wouldn't go far. He was wrong. Knowing other hunters were in the area, Tony got on the track immediately. He followed it for 200 yards before finding a bloodied bed. Thankfully, the forest was blanketed in snow, and that made the tracking job a bit easier. However, he soon realized he was tracking a gut-shot deer. Years of experience have taught us to stay off the track of a gut-shot deer for at least 10 hours, but we sometimes have to break that rule when hunting in highly pressured areas. What's more, the day's forecast called for more snow. Tony knew he'd need help if he were to recover his buck, so he headed back to camp and waited 3 hours. The crew came back at 11 a.m. and took up the trail. Their plan was simple: One hunter would stay on the track while one stayed back at the last sign of blood. The third hunter carried a rifle and walked ahead of the trackers with his eyes focused on the cover in hopes of spotting the buck in its bed. They tracked the deer several hundred yards and found two more beds. However, by 2 p.m., they weren't any closer to finding the deer. Still, they vowed to stick it out till the bitter end. The trail continued up ridges and through swamps. Finally, it cut across the gravel road that passed my dad's lakeside cabin – spanning more than 2 miles. I would have never believed it had I not walked it myself after the fact.

At 3 p.m., the gang gathered at the last spot of blood by the lakeshore. They were completely whipped. Some were ready to quit. Tony stood silently, removed his knit hat and wiped his brow. "Let's be patient," he said. After a short break, the hunters walked the shoreline to look for more clues. Seconds later, Tony saw a dark object atop an ice reef on the other side of the lake … it was his buck! Amazingly, the dying buck had enough left in him to swim 300 yards before collapsing on that reef. I had been hunting an area not too far away when I heard the hoots and hollers echoing across the lake. I instantly climbed from my stand and headed back to camp. When I got there, one of the hunters was rowing our aluminum boat to shore with Tony's buck tied to the transom. "How on earth did you get that buck?" I asked. "We never gave up," Tony replied.

I realize some folks might be bothered by the fact that Tony's shot didn't put the buck down in its tracks. Indeed, as responsible hunters, we always strive to make a quick, clean kill. This isn't a perfect world. Mistakes sometimes happen. However, I believe a lot can be learned from such incidents. In this instance, which took place decades ago, we learned to avoid taking snap shots at deer. We also learned to never give up on a wounded animal.

Coyote Concerns

The coyote is perhaps the most-maligned deer predator in the woods. Hunters blame them for everything from low deer densities to reduced populations of mature bucks. The fact is coyotes kill some deer, but they do not pose serious threats to the well-being of most free-ranging deer herds. There are some exceptions, including areas of the Southwest and far North, but they are few and far between.

The coyote, however, is extremely efficient at finding wounded deer, and, for that matter, is a force to be reckoned with when deciding when and where to trail hunter-shot whitetails. Although some blood-trailing rules call for hunters to wait before trailing wounded deer, all bets are off (except on gut shots) when you're hunting areas thick with coyotes.

This topic is extremely fresh in my mind as I write these words, because I lost a deer to coyotes just days ago. I was bowhunting in Brown County, Ill., which is part of the famous Golden Triangle region. It was the fourth day of my rut-time hunt, and action was slow. I hadn't seen a deer in 2 days but was alerted to the sounds of hoofsteps in the dry leaves as the sun inched toward the horizon. It was a monster doe, and she was being followed by her two fawns. The landowner had encouraged us to shoot some does to help with his management program, so I quickly clipped my release onto the bowstring and prepared for the shot.

The doe picked at browse for nearly 10 minutes until she finally stepped into shooting range. The arrow left my bow so fast that I didn't even see it hit her. She skipped a few yards, flicked her tail, then trotted about 40 yards before stopping to survey the surroundings. Had I not heard the arrow hit her, I would have sworn I blew it. The doe then walked a few more yards before I lost sight of her. Chattering fox squirrels made it difficult for me to hear much, but I thought I heard the doe crash about a minute later. However, I wasn't sure, so I stayed put and waited for darkness.

After climbing from my stand, I tiptoed to the spot where the doe had been standing and found my arrow with light streaks of blood on it. I left it there and backed out so I could discuss the situation with my guide. He decided we should wait a few hours, "just in case." Well, you can guess what happened next. After waiting just 3 hours, we picked up the blood trail and followed it a scant 100 yards … to my dead doe that had already been picked apart by coyotes. I can't describe how disappointed I was; it was as if someone had stolen one of my tree stands or something. Despite having the same thing happen during a muzzleloading hunt 2 years earlier, I still felt sick to my stomach.

Coyotes have a knack for finding mortally wounded deer, but their success rates can be hit or miss. During that same trip in which I lost the doe, three hunters shot deer that had to be left overnight. All three were recovered without incident.

Why do coyotes find some wounded deer so quickly yet miss out on others? That's a question even prominent researchers have trouble answering. The best guess is that coyotes merely happen to be in the right place at the right time. Some researchers assert that high coyote densities – not the predator's keen sense of smell – is the biggest reason why hunters in some areas lose a higher percentage of their deer than those in other areas. That seemed to hold true for the Illinois river-bottom country I was hunting, because during the first 3 days I saw more coyotes (five) than deer while hunting.

"You've got to understand that coyotes become very familiar with the habitat, especially river bottoms," Cabela's Mark Nelsen once told me. Nelsen, a former employee of the Nebraska Game and Parks Commission, should know. He routinely hunts whitetails in Nebraska's river-bottom country, which is also home to some of the highest coyote populations in the U.S. "They hunt it the same way a human would," he continued. "At night, they are constantly cruising the perimeter of the cover to pick up scent. They use the same trails that deer and humans use. As a result, they form a routine, and they run it practically every day."

To improve your odds of recovering a deer in coyote country, follow a few simple rules:

1. Organize a search party and stay on the blood trail all night if needed, especially if you are trailing a deer you know is mortally wounded. Do not use this tactic on gut-shot deer. Always wait 10 to 12 hours before trailing any gut-shot deer. This is one exception that must be made, because a gut-shot deer can easily travel a mile or more if pushed.

2. Use human scent to your advantage. If you must leave a deer overnight, intentionally contaminate the area with human scent. Hang jackets, hats, gloves, etc. in the area. Some hunters even urinate in several locations in the area where their wounded deer ran. The tactic isn't foolproof, but it can keep scent-conscious coyotes out of the area long enough to buy you some time.

3. Where legal, use a trailing dog. Coyotes aren't always afraid of dogs, but, again, the mere presence of a hound in the woods might spook coyotes enough to keep them from finding your deer before you do.

4. If you find your deer but must leave it in the woods until you can get help dragging it out, hang it in a tree. Get it far enough off the ground to keep coyotes and other scavengers from picking away at the hams, tenderloins, etc.

An Extra Step
Take Time To Reflect

I s it just me, or have we really gotten greedy about the whitetails that roam our swamps, fields and forests? Excuse me for being blunt, but I think I'm going to be ill if I hear one more person possessively refer to a free-ranging deer herd. You have probably heard it, too:

"Those public-land hunters are killing all *my* deer!" ... or

"We no longer do deer drives because we might push all of *our* big bucks onto the neighbors' land!" ... or

"Don't plant food plots near your property lines. Otherwise, everyone else will be shooting *your* deer."

What kind of message are such statements sending future generations? OK, so you've worked hard, saved money and bought land, obtained a lease or gained exclusive access somewhere. You've also invested a lot of time and money to chase that sportsman's dream ... a mature buck of wall-hanging proportions. There's nothing wrong with that. It's what makes America great.

Still, it's important to remember that selfishness is not God's way. In fact, it's one of the Seven Heresies. If you truly care about your fellow man, take a step back and ponder what's really important in this life. And, while you're at it, brush up on a few of those Commandments that are no longer allowed to be displayed in public places.

Since I'm perched on the stump, I'd also like to take a moment to reiterate a point I made on the pages of *Deer & Deer Hunting* not so long ago. It has to do with humility and respect.

Each year, I come in contact with hundreds of great deer hunters. I talk with them on the phone, exchange e-mails, and meet them at gas stations, deer shows and at various camps across this great land. For the most part, they're hard-working, fun-loving people who truly respect the land and the animals they hunt. However, over the years, I've noticed a disturbing trend. I can't really put my finger on it, but it seems to me that many hunters have stepped off the path of righteousness. I don't believe it was a sharply defined turn, but rather a gentle meandering that occurred over the course of several generations.

In general, I believe modern hunters don't truly appreciate the animals we kill. Maybe we're spoiled by today's record deer herds. Maybe our comfortable lifestyles have detached our souls from all things wild.

Maybe we just don't care.

Minimally, all deer hunters should be thankful for a venison bounty. Most of us are. However, how many of us truly respect the deer we kill? How many of us stand in quiet deliberation over a fallen whitetail? How many take a moment to ponder our own existence? This isn't about religion. It's about respect.

Canada's Cree Indians were especially reverent to slain animals. In fact, their entire hunting tradition was built on elaborate rules honoring slain creatures. A hunter's post-hunt behavior was at the top of the list. Hunters were forbidden from over-celebrating their kills. In fact, even unintentional boasts of a hunter's prowess were thought to insult animal spirits and bring bad luck.

All deer hunters should be thankful for a venison bounty.

Hunters in American tribes followed similar rules, and they made sure the remains of every deer were respected. It was customary for many tribes to prop a buck's head – and antlers – in the crotch of a tree so the buck's "spirit" could watch sunrises and sunsets. They also believed this reassured other animals that they needn't be afraid of yielding their bodies to humans. Other tribes were careful to utilize the entire animal, including every scrap of meat from the carcass.

I use these examples not to advocate pantheism – the belief that all things are God – but to illustrate how far modern man is detached from the earth. I don't believe taking photos of dead deer or getting a buck's head mounted is irreverent. If anything, those acts honor the animals. However, we can rest assured the Cree never placed sunglasses on deer heads, hung a buck's testicles in a tree or bragged about how they "stuck" a doe. Furthermore, I doubt an American Indian ever partially skinned a fawn, then – out of pure laziness – cut out the backstraps and left the rest to rot.

A college professor once told me that irreverence toward dead creatures is common among people who are anxious about their own mortality. He also said it often takes but one reminder to trigger the necessary guilt to right one's internal compass. Looking at today's world makes me wonder if primitive hunters possessed a far greater understanding of the natural world than their modern counterparts.

Index

PHOTO CREDITS:

All photos by author, with these exceptions:

Tracy Schmidt photos: pages 31, 120, 123 (bottom), 129, 185.

Charles Alsheimer photos: Pages 10, 12, 16, 36, 41, 56, 70, 80, 101, 113, 121 (top), 122, 123 (top), 124, 125 (top), 126, 131, 132, 145, 148, 150, 220 and 221.

Pat Reeve photos: Pages 27, 28, 46, 61, 68, 81, 82, 92, 118, 182, 211 and 218.

Photos on pages 17, 86 and 140 courtesy of Laura Seitz Inc.

INDEX